CLASSIC

WHODUNITS

MORE THAN 100 MYSTERIES FOR YOU TO SOLVE!

CLASSIC
WHODUNITS

MORE THAN 100 MYSTERIES FOR YOU TO SOLVE!

BY TOM BULLIMORE, HY CONRAD,
DERRICK NIEDERMAN, STAN SMITH

STERLING INNOVATION®
An imprint of Sterling Publishing Co., Inc.

New York / London
www.sterlingpublishing.com

STERLING and the distinctive Sterling logo are registered trademarks of Sterling Publishing Co., Inc.

Library of Congress Cataloging-in-Publication Data Available

10 9 8 7 6 5

Published by Sterling Publishing Co., Inc.
387 Park Avenue South, New York, NY 10016
© 2003, 2008 by Sterling Publishing Co., Inc.

Material in this collection was adapted from
Five-Minute Whodunits © 1997 Stanley Smith
Sherlock Holmes' Puzzles of Deduction © 1997 by Tom Bullimore
Inspector Forsooth's Whodunits © 1998 by Derrick Niederman
Whodunit Crime Puzzles © 2002 by Hy Conrad and Tatjana Mai Wyss

Distributed in Canada by Sterling Publishing
$^{c}/o$ Canadian Manda Group, 165 Dufferin Street,
Toronto, Ontario, Canada M6K 3H6
Distributed in the United Kingdom by GMC Distribution Services
Castle Place, 166 High Street, Lewes, East Sussex, England BN7 1XU
Distributed in Australia by Capricorn Link (Australia) Pty. Ltd.
P.O. Box 704, Windsor, NSW 2756, Australia

Printed in China
All rights reserved

Sterling ISBN: 978-1-4027-6009-9

For information about custom editions, special sales, premium and corporate purchases, please contact Sterling Special Sales Department at 800-805-5489 or specialsales@sterlingpublishing.com.

CLASSIC WHODUNITS

CONTENTS

INTRODUCTION

Do you love a twisty mystery—the locked room, the impossible crime, the pivotal piece of evidence that appears to make no sense even though it has to? Do you love it when the writer plays with your mind, but plays fair, and you get to slowly turn the story inside out and finally discover that elegantly simple twist?

The traditional "whodunit" does not hinge on police techniques, trivia, or even pure logic. It is based on imagination, is clever, and never too annoyingly complex. This book is chock full of many such puzzlers, with the added perk that it invites you—the reader—to join up with and work shoulder to shoulder with some expert crime-solvers.

A crime has been committed, and it is up to you to untangle the evidence and find the guilty party. Of course, as you'll discover, it may not be that simple. There's usually a twist. Was the murder a frame-up? Was a murder made to look like a suicide? Was there a break-in, or was it an inside job? Does that "innocent" bystander bear up under scrutiny, or is something more devious going on?

Examine the clues one at a time, and try to digest each clue before you consider the next. Mull over the evidence and try to make sense of it. If your budding theory fails to address all the concerns, then return to the account of the crime. Take your time in reviewing the case, and try to tie up all those loose ends before you finally look up the solution in the back.

Classic whodunits rank among the purest forms of puzzle; they ask you to make delicious sense out of what's seemingly contradictory. So, relax and enjoy the challenges ahead as you match wits with some of the best!

MATCH WITS WITH SHERMAN OLIVER HOLMES

MEET YOUR COLLEAGUE

No one knew where Sherman Oliver Holmes came from or how he'd gotten his money. One day, Capital City was just your run-of-the-mill metropolitan area. The next day, a short, rotund millionaire in a deerstalker cap began showing up at crime scenes, claiming to be the great-great-grandson of Sherlock Holmes and offering his expert opinion.

Sergeant Gunther Wilson of the Major Crimes Division was irritated by how often this eccentric little man with the southern drawl would appear within minutes of a grisly murder and stick his nose into official police business. What disturbed Wilson even more was the fact that this eccentric little man was nearly always right.

"The loony should be committed," Wilson had been heard to say on more than one occasion. "He always has some outlandish theory. I'd sign the commitment papers myself—if

I didn't have a soft spot for him." But Wilson didn't have a soft spot. What he did have was a phenomenal record for solving cases, thanks in large part to his "loony" friend.

To his credit, Sherman wasn't much interested in taking credit. As far as the public was concerned, the Capital City police were simply doing a better job than ever before. So Sergeant Wilson decided to swallow his pride and befriend the exasperating, unique little gentleman who had nothing better to do than pop up like a fat rabbit and do the work of an entire detective squad.

THE MISSING MONET

Sherman Holmes didn't know how he did it; but he did, and on a regular basis. Sometimes he'd see a police cruiser and stop to see what was happening. Sometimes he'd follow the sound of a siren. More often than not, he would just be walking or driving around Capital City when a sixth sense would tell him to turn here or stop there.

It was this sixth sense for crime that brought him to the Hudson Office Building on a blustery March day. Sherman settled quietly into a chair in the lobby, patiently waiting for something to happen.

The first visitor to catch his eye was a bike messenger, arriving with a package-filled backpack and a long document tube. The messenger disappeared into an express elevator labeled 31st Floor. Five minutes later, the messenger reappeared and left the building, still carrying the tube but one package lighter.

Taking his place in the elevator was an elegantly attired man, an older gentleman, using a cane as he limped heavily on his left leg.

The gentleman reappeared in the lobby ten minutes later. On his exit from the elevator he nearly collided with a woman in a Gucci suit. The umbrella in her left hand became momentarily entangled with the cane in his right.

"Watch where you're going," she snapped.

"My apologies," he replied.

The man limped off and the woman pressed her button and fidgeted with her umbrella until the elevator door closed. Her visit lasted five minutes.

Sherman was beginning to think his crime-sensing instincts were flawed. Perhaps it was this nasty cold he was just getting over. Then a pair of police officers rushed into the lobby and took the same express elevator to the 31st floor. "It's about time they called in the police," Sherman said with satisfaction.

When they left the building a half hour later, Sherman followed them to the Baker Street Coffee Shop. He slipped into the booth behind theirs, quietly ordered an English muffin, and eavesdropped.

"What was a million-dollar painting doing in the reception area?" the older cop asked his partner. Sherman recognized him as Sergeant Gunther Wilson, an officer he'd chatted with at dozens of other crime scenes.

The 31st floor, it seems, contained the offices of the Hudson Company's top brass, and the furnishings in the reception area included a small Monet oil, about one foot square. Only three visitors had been alone there long enough to cut the painting out of its frame—a bike messenger delivering documents, the ne'er-do-well uncle of the company president wanting to borrow a few dollars, and the vice president's estranged wife, who had come to complain about her allowance. All three had visited the offices before and could have previously noticed the unguarded painting.

"Excuse me," Sherman said as he rose from his booth and ambled up to Officer Wilson and his partner.

Wilson saw the pudgy little man in his deerstalker cap and frock-coat and beamed. "Sherlock Holmes, I presume."

"That was my great-great-grandfather," Sherman answered politely. "But I did inherit a few of his modest powers. Would you like me to tell you who stole that painting?"

WHO STOLE THE PAINTING?
WHAT CLUE GAVE THE THIEF AWAY?

Solution on page 229.

A MAZE OF SUSPECTS

Sherman Holmes was out for a drive on a lonely country road. He saw the police car and the sign for the labyrinth maze at almost the same moment. "A labyrinth puzzle plus a crime," he chuckled, stepping on the brakes. "How lovely." He switched on his turn signal and pulled off into the parking lot.

The roadside attraction, "Queen Victoria's Maze," consisted of a ticket booth, a small, shabby office, and the maze itself, a seven-foot-high square of ill-kept hedges. Curious motorists were lured into paying three dollars apiece to get lost in the confusing pathways inside the hedges.

Sherman bypassed the empty ticket booth and wandered up a gravel path and into the maze itself. Two right turns brought him

to a dead end—a dead end complete with a corpse.
A highway patrolman was standing over the
corpse of a casually dressed man, a knife
stuck between his ribs. Three men and a
woman faced the officer.

"My husband Kyle and I came into the
maze and split up just for fun," the woman said
between sobs. "After several minutes of wandering, I
wound up outside at another entrance. I was going to try again. I
called Kyle, to see how he was doing. That's when I heard it—
some scuffling—like a fight. Then Kyle screamed."

"I heard the scream, too," said the tallest man. "I was on a
bench at the center of the maze. I didn't hear any scuffling, probably because the fountain there drowned it out. I'm Bill McQuire. I
hurried out of the maze and found Mrs. Turner. The two of us
went back in and discovered the body together."

"I'm the owner," said a short, disheveled man. "Paul Moran.
These people were the only three customers in there. After taking
the Turners' money at the ticket booth, I went into the office. Abe,
my electrician, was rewiring the system. I switched off the main
fuse box for him. Then I walked around picking up trash. Abe was
still working when I heard a man's scream."

Abe, the electrician, was the last to speak. "What Paul said is
true. I was in a crawl space under the office the whole time, doing
the wiring. I didn't see anything or hear anyone until the scream."

The officer bent down to examine the body. "No wallet. Maybe
it was a botched robbery. But we'll have to wait for the experts."

"I'm an expert," came a voice from behind. They turned

around to find a short, owlish man with a briar pipe between his teeth. "Sherman Holmes, at your service. The solution is elementary, if you'd care to listen."

WHO KILLED KYLE TURNER?
HOW DID SHERMAN DEDUCE THE TRUTH?

Solution on page 230.

BUS STATION BOMBER

"Where have you been?" Sergeant Wilson stepped around the burned and mangled debris of what had been the rear wall of the Capital City bus terminal. "I thought you must be sick."

Gunther Wilson was secretly dependent on Sherman Holmes's habit of showing up uninvited at crime scenes. He certainly wasn't used to waiting three hours for the odd, pudgy millionaire to make an appearance.

"Sorry, old man." Sherman sniffled. "I haven't been myself. Spring allergies."

Wilson pointed to a four-man squad arranging charred bits of metal on a white sheet. "The bomb was in a locker. It went off at three p.m. There were a few injuries, but nothing serious. The mechanism was an old wind-up clock wired to two sticks of dynamite. It was triggered by the alarm mechanism hitting the '3'."

"Do you have a motive?"

"Not a clue. My guess is he did it for the thrill, like some of the sick arsonists we've dealt with lately."

"Let's hope we catch him before he tries again." Sherman glanced around the terminal. "Did anyone see who used the locker?"

"I got in touch with the night clerk." Wilson waved over a slight, sleepy-looking man. "Mr. Pollard, tell my associate what you saw."

"Certainly." Andy Pollard adjusted his thick eyeglasses and cleared his throat. "Last night as I was coming in to work, around two a.m., I saw this cabdriver parking out front. He walked in with a red travel bag and put it in that locker."

Wilson waved again and two more men crossed to join them.

"We checked with the cab companies. Only two taxis were in the area around two a.m. Unfortunately, Mr. Pollard can't identify the driver."

"I remember the red bag," Pollard apologized, "but not the guy's face."

The first driver was a tall, fair-haired lad, barely out of high school.

"I've been driving for about a month," he explained. "I picked up a passenger at the airport and dropped her off at the hotel on the corner. That was around two. Then I filled up at the gas station on Highland and ended my shift. If this guy says I came in here, he's lying. I haven't been in a bus station in years."

The second driver was around the same height but middle-aged and with a pronounced gut hanging over his belt. "I dropped off a fare in front of the terminal," he told them. "My fare said he'd left his car in the parking lot earlier in the day and had to pick it up. That was a few minutes after two.

"Then my dispatcher sent me to a bar on Fifth to pick up a drunk. No one was there. A man waved me down and I took him to an all-night diner on Swann Street. It's all in my log book if you don't believe me."

One of the members of the bomb squad was standing by, waiting for a chance to speak. "Excuse me, Sarge," he said. "The container was a red bag, just like the witness said. A red leather satchel."

"Thanks," Wilson said, then turned to Sherman and shrugged. "Not much to go on, huh?"

"Just enough to give us the bomber," Sherman purred. "I can't tell you why he did it, but I can certainly tell you who."

WHO BOMBED THE BUS STATION?
WHAT FACT CLUED SHERMAN IN?

Solution on page 230.

THE POSTMAN RINGS ONCE

Sergeant Wilson found the letter and envelope torn up and crammed into the bottom of a wastebasket. Reassembling it while wearing plastic gloves proved difficult.

"It's from Henry Liggit's lawyer," he finally said, looking up from the jigsaw-like puzzle. "It outlines Mr. Liggit's proposed new will, disinheriting his three nephews and leaving everything to charity."

Sherman stood behind the sergeant, peering over his shoulder. "What do you think?" Wilson asked him.

"Hmm. It doesn't take a Sherman Holmes," said Sherman Holmes, "to suspect that Mr. Liggit's suicide wasn't really a suicide."

"My thoughts exactly," the officer agreed.

Sherman and the sergeant were in Henry Liggit's library, just yards from where the millionaire lay slumped in his chair with a gun in his hand and a hole in his head.

"Our first job, my dear Wilson, will be determining which devoted nephew opened Liggit's mail and discovered the threat to his inheritance." With that, Sherman led the way into the front hall where the nervous nephews stood waiting.

All three nephews lived in the Liggit house; all three had been at home at the time of the shot. None, or so they swore, had the least idea Uncle Henry had been about to cut them out of his will.

"Uncle Henry had been depressed," said Nigel, the eldest, in mournful tones. He was sipping a martini and Sherman suspected it wasn't his first of the day. "I spent all afternoon at home. About three p.m. I walked into the front hall. I was checking the mail on that side table when I heard the gunshot."

Sherman observed a few pieces of mail on the table. "When did the mail arrive, my good fellows?"

Gerald, the youngest nephew, raised his hand. "When I got home around 2:30, the mail was already on the hall floor. I walked right across it before noticing. I picked it up and put it on the hall table."

"Did you check through it?"

Gerald nodded. "Yes, but there was nothing for me. I went straight out to the garden and sat by the pool. I, too, heard the gunshot. Around three, as Nigel said."

"I looked through the mail," volunteered the middle nephew, Thomas. "I'd just got home from a trip I put my bags down in the hall, sorted through, and found a letter for me. I put it in my pocket, then went up to my room."

"What time was this?"

"Ten minutes to three, or thereabouts. I was unpacking when I heard the shot."

"Is the letter still in your pocket?"

With some hesitation, Thomas reached into his jacket and produced the unopened envelope. Sherman noticed a faint shoe print, a water ring, and a curious return address. "It's from a bill collector," Thomas confessed. "I've got a cash flow problem."

"Can anyone verify your arrival at the house at 2:50?"

"I can," said Gerald. "You can see the driveway from poolside. Thomas's car pulled in about ten minutes before poor Uncle killed himself."

"Yes," said Sherman. "We'll talk about suicide in a minute. Did any of you notice a letter addressed to your uncle from his lawyer?"

The nephews all shook their heads.

"Then that settles it," said Sherman. "One of you is lying. One of you knew about your uncle's plans to change his will and killed him before he could do it."

"I don't know what you're talking about," said Nigel.

"Join the club," laughed Sergeant Wilson. "I don't know what he's talking about half the time, either. But he's usually right."

WHO KILLED HENRY LIGGIT?
WHAT PROOF DOES SHERMAN HAVE?

Solution on page 231.

FOUL BALL BURGLARY

Sherman Holmes sat on a park bench, watching as the neighborhood boys played a pick-up game of baseball. "I should retrieve my great-great-grandfather's bat and teach those lads the art of cricket," the amateur detective thought, then realized he didn't know how to play it himself.

"Oh, well," he sighed. "The lads are awfully close to those houses." And that, of course, was the exact moment when the batter hit a long fly in just that direction. Glass shattered and a home alarm began to wail.

The left fielder, a boy called Jake, went after the ball. He scrambled up a high wooden fence and straddled the top, gazing at the house and yard below. "The ball broke a window, all right," he

shouted back to the others. Then his eyes widened. "Hey—you better call the police. I think there's been a robbery."

The game broke up immediately. Jake lowered himself into the backyard while the other boys circled around to the front of the house and awaited the police.

Jake unlocked the door from inside and let the officers in. Sherman sneaked in right behind. The rotund little Southerner was safely ensconced behind a potted palm when a man and a woman drove up in separate cars.

The newcomers joined the police inside. Sherman edged his potted palm into a good viewing position and managed to piece together the essentials.

The newcomers were brother and sister, Larry and Laura Conners. The house had belonged to their late father, who kept his coin collection on display on a table by the rear garden window. This was what Jake must have seen from the fence. The heavy table lay on its side, not far from the wayward baseball. Remnants of the broken window were everywhere. A patrolman walked across the fallen tablecloth and Sherman could hear the muted crunch of glass under the white linen.

The Conners both had keys and both knew the alarm code. They had been here together just this morning, arguing about the coins.

"Laura must've come back and stolen them," snarled Larry. "Then she overturned the table in some pathetic attempt to blame it on a burglar. I was at home, ten miles from here, washing my car. My neighbors saw me. I was there right up until you called me."

Laura glared at her brother. "I was at home, too, eight miles in the other direction. I was on the phone with Aunt Doreen and doing my laundry. You can check with her if you want to."

Sherman wanted to jump out from behind the palm and instantly solve the case. But that might seem a little odd. So he restrained himself and waited until the officers were leaving.

WHO STOLE THE COINS?
WHAT CLUE POINTS TO THE THIEF?

Solution on page 232.

THE UNSAFE SAFE HOUSE

For all the help Sherman Holmes provided the police, he received little if any recognition. In fact, the officers he helped the most were often the first to make fun of his quirky personality. "They don't want people thinking some amateur is solving their cases," Sherman would say with a generous shrug. "I just wish I didn't have to sneak around eavesdropping all the time."

One of Sherman's most extreme eavesdropping cases involved hiding behind a coatrack for over an hour. On that day, his instincts for crime led him beyond a yellow-tape barricade and into the front hall of a police safe house, a normal-looking home in a modest, pleasant-looking row house in which a mob witness had just been murdered.

From behind the safety of the coats, Sherman watched as a nervous rookie stood over the body of the strangled man. A minute later, Captain Loeb strode in, his baggy suit flapping in the breeze.

"I was here protecting the witness," stammered the rookie. "Then I got a call from your office, ordering me back to the station. I left him alone. By the time I figured out the call was a fake and rushed back here, Frankie was dead."

The captain remained calm. "Who all has keys to the front door?"

"Just me," answered the rookie. "The door locked automatically behind me. I told Frankie not to open up to anyone."

Captain Loeb examined the body. "Strangled from behind, meaning he probably trusted his assailant. Who would Frankie open the door for? Let's get them in here."

The first suspect to be brought in was Lou, the victim's brother-in-law. "Frankie sneaked a telephone call to me last night at work," Lou said, staring down at the corpse. "I'm a phone company operator. Frankie didn't tell me where he was. My wife is going to go nuts when she hears."

The second suspect was Barry Aiello, the secret mob informant who had talked Frankie into testifying. "I feel like I'm responsible," he sighed. "The mob was using all their contacts to find him." Barry bent down and examined the welts around the victim's neck. "Looks like a belt was used. Poor Frankie shouldn't have turned his back."

Captain Loeb had them both taken in for questioning, then crossed to the rack and grabbed his trench coat. "The commissioner's gonna have my head, but I suppose I gotta call him." Loeb had just pulled a notepad from his coat pocket when he saw a face staring out from behind Frankie's leather jacket. "Who in blazes are you?"

"Hi!" Sherman was so nervous, he momentarily forgot his English accent. "I'm so sorry. I know I'm trespassing, but..." He could think of only one way to redeem himself, and that was to hand them Frankie's killer.

WHO KILLED FRANKIE?
WHAT TIPPED SHERMAN OFF?

Solution on page 233.

THE CRYSTAL VANISHES

Luther brought a new pot of coffee into the dining room and began refreshing everyone's cup. "Agatha, is that the crystal ball you were telling us about?"

"Isn't it gorgeous!" The young woman in the flowing robe held it up for all to see, a round piece of cut crystal, not much larger than a baseball. "The salesman guaranteed me that it once belonged to Morgan LeFay. And this wasn't her everyday crystal either. It was her special one." Agatha passed the ball to Sherman Holmes.

"It's blooming lovely," Sherman said, managing to keep a straight face. He enjoyed his weekly dinners with Luther, Agatha, and Grimelda. The warlock and two witches might seem a little extreme to Sherman's other friends, but they were full of life and always interesting. And they accepted without question Sherman's own idiosyncrasies.

All three examined the ball, then watched as Agatha returned it to the red velvet box. "They say it has a mind of its own. If the crystal doesn't like its current owner, it will find a new one. We get along swimmingly, I'm glad to say."

The evening was almost over. Agatha helped Luther, the host, clear the dining room table, while Grimelda went to the bathroom and Sherman browsed through Luther's library. When he returned to the living room, Grimelda was adjusting her shawl and checking her makeup in the mirror over the mantle. She had always been the most attractive witch in the coven. Sherman had heard from Luther that there was some tension between her and the younger, newer arrival, Agatha.

"Next week at my abode," Sherman reminded her.

Grimelda seemed startled. "Oh, that's right. We're going to help you contact Dr. Watson. We never had much luck contacting your great-great-grandfather, did we?"

"We'll have to keep trying. Luther!" he shouted to the next room. "A scrumptious dinner." Then he saw the velvet box on the sideboard beside the full pot of coffee. "Agatha, don't forget your crystal." Sherman picked up the box and could instantly tell it was too light.

"It's gone," Agatha cried when she discovered the empty box. "Morgan's crystal has left me. I feel so rejected!"

"Oh, that's too bad," Grimelda commiserated. Luther agreed. The three witches seemed quite willing to accept the crystal's disappearance as a natural phenomenon. But Sherman knew better.

WHO TOOK THE CRYSTAL BALL?
WHERE IS IT HIDDEN?

Solution on page 234.

THE POINTING CORPSE

When the detective business was slow, the great Sherlock Holmes had spent the long, empty hours playing the violin. Sherman Holmes did the same, but with less soothing results. "Maybe I should take lessons," he would think as he sawed back and forth across the strings. When things got really slow, Sherman switched on one of his police band radios.

After two boring days of drizzle and inactivity, the detective intercepted a call reporting a murder victim found in a car. Sherman happened to be driving his classic Bentley at the time and made a quick turn up High Canyon Road.

He arrived to find Gunther Wilson standing between his patrol car and a white sedan parked beside a panoramic view. The sergeant actually looked glad to see him. "I'm a little out of my depth on this one," he said. "It's a celebrity, Mervin Hightower. Shot at

close range. I'm waiting for forensics and a tow truck. On top of being murdered, his car battery's dead."

The whole city knew Mervin Hightower, a newspaper columnist who specialized in scandalous exposés. Sherman walked around to the driver's side. An arm extended out the partially open window, propped up on the glass edge. The hand was made

into a fist, except for the index finger, which was straight and firm with rigor mortis.

"He appears to be pointing," Sherman deduced. "How long has the fellow been dead?"

"What do I look like, a clock? The forensics boys will narrow it down. I saw the car and stopped to see if he needed help, which he doesn't. I recognized him, even with the blood."

Sherman looked in to see the columnist's familiar face contorted and frozen in agony. "I presume the man survived for a minute after the attack. What do you think he was pointing at, old bean? Something that could identify his killer?" Sherman lined up his eyes along the extended arm. "What story was he working on?"

Wilson pulled a newspaper from his back pocket. "Here. In today's column, he says he's going to expose some embezzlement from the City Charity Board."

"There are only three people on the Charity Board," Sherman said, checking the column for their names. "Marilyn Lake, Arthur Curtis, and Tony Pine." Then he examined the view: a glistening lake, a neon sign for Curtis Furniture and a majestic grove of evergreens. "Zounds!"

"Zounds is right. If Mervin was trying to point out his killer, he did a lousy job."

"Not necessarily." Sherman was thinking. "I think he did just fine."

WHO KILLED MERVIN HIGHTOWER?
HOW DID SHERMAN KNOW?

Solution on page 234.

BELL, BOOKE, OR KENDALL?

"My regrets, Wilson. I have no idea who killed him."

"What?" Sergeant Wilson thought he would never hear Sherman Holmes say those words. He wasn't too happy about it, either. "Okay, okay, calm down." Wilson sounded close to panic himself. "Mr. Boren, maybe you should review the facts."

Sherman and the sergeant were in the downtown offices of Boren Technologies, a designer of handheld computers. Arvin Boren sat at his desk, eyeing the professional detective and the eccentric amateur. "Someone's been stealing our designs. My vice president, Don Silver, and I kept the problem secret. And we narrowed the suspects down to three." He pointed out the window of his private office to where a skinny kid in shirtsleeves was stuffing yellow envelopes into a mail slot.

"That's Wally Bell, an intern from City College. He does a lot of our copying and binding, so he has access to our priority documents. The heavyset guy sitting outside my office, that's Solly Booke, my assistant. He's sending his son to private school. I don't know where he gets the money.

"The third possibility is Inez Kendall." A young woman in a tasteful, expensive suit was tacking a newspaper article to a bulletin board right next to the elevators. "Inez is director of public relations. She has the most contact with our competitors."

Sherman nodded. "Was it Mr. Silver's idea to try to trap the traitor?"

"I'm afraid so," Boren sighed. "We're developing a new version of our Wrist 2002. Don left the plans lying conspicuously on his desk. The thief never took originals, only copies. Don planned to hide in the copy room and catch the guy. Only the guy must have caught him."

Sergeant Wilson took over the narrative. "Silver was killed in the copy room by a blow to the head. Mr. Boren and an associate found the body almost immediately. All three suspects were immediately sequestered and their possessions searched. We haven't been able to locate the plans."

Sherman took the sergeant across to the window but didn't lower his voice. "The thief couldn't afford to be caught with them. My guess is the plans got thrown down that mail slot. It's the only place they could be."

Five minutes later, Sergeant Wilson persuaded a maintenance man to open the ground-floor mail chute. There the plans were, nestled right on top of a layer of yellow envelopes. "Just as I thought," Sherman said, turning to Wilson. "Now I know the killer."

WHO KILLED DON SILVER?
HOW DID SHERMAN KNOW?

Solution on page 235.

THE WAYWARD WILL

Sherman Holmes signed his name to the will and then watched as Harmon Grove signed as the other witness. "Thanks for dropping over—again," the congenial lawyer said as he slipped the will into his briefcase. "The Fielding kids can't be witnesses because they inherit."

"Not a problem," Sherman replied. This was the fourth time he had been asked over to witness a new version of Jacob Fielding's will. "You get better now, Jake," Sherman said to the frail man propped up in bed. Jacob nodded weakly and closed his eyes.

Sherman and the lawyer walked out into the hall. "This may be

the old man's last will," Harmon whispered. "I don't expect he'll last the night." Solemn-faced, Anna passed them and entered the sick room.

There were three Fielding children. As their next-door neighbor, Sherman knew them well—Anna, the nurse; Brock, now a surgeon at a local hospital; and Keith, fresh out of college. All three had moved back into the family home during their father's long, difficult illness.

Harmon deposited his briefcase on the dining room table, and walked Sherman to the door. As they entered the foyer, Anna appeared at the top of the stairs. "Mr. Grove, I think . . . I think he's dead."

The two men joined the Fielding children who had already gathered in the dead man's bedroom. Brock checked for vital signs, then gently pulled the sheet over his father's face.

Half an hour later, as the people from the funeral home were removing the body, Sherman and Harmon once more crossed through the dining room. Harmon saw his briefcase and eyed it curiously. "It's been moved," he said, then opened the leather lid. "The new will. It's gone!"

Sherman and the lawyer backtracked their movements through the bedroom, dining room, and hall, hoping to find the will somehow mislaid. Finally they had no choice but to assemble the bereaved children and treat them as suspects.

"I went downstairs once after he died," Anna claimed. "To get the number for the funeral home. I called them from the kitchen. I didn't go into the dining room, and I certainly didn't touch your briefcase."

"I went downstairs to let the funeral people in," Dr. Brock Fielding said. "I saw the briefcase but didn't touch it. I didn't even know the will was in there."

Keith sighed. "Well, I didn't go downstairs at all. After Brock declared father dead, I returned to my room to call some relatives. What do we do if we can't find the will?"

"We'll have to use his last will," Harmon explained. "It's almost exactly the same. You know how eccentric he was. All three of you still get substantial bequests. He left me the same token gift. Plus small amounts go to servants and employees."

"I can find the new will," Sherman said softly. The others all turned, a little surprised to find him still in the room. "I think I know where to look."

WHERE IS THE WILL NOW?
HOW DID SHERMAN KNOW WHERE TO LOOK?

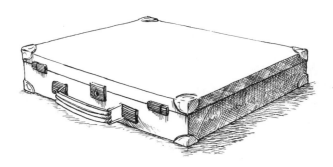

Solution on page 236.

THE DOC'S LAST LUNCH

Sergeant Wilson hated stakeouts. Here he was, stuck alone in a first-floor apartment, photographing the comings and goings at the home of a suspected hit man across the street. And it was a beautiful day outside, which just made things worse.

Wilson heard the door to his own apartment building close and glanced outside to see Dr. Weber's regular Tuesday patient leaving. 11:58, he noted on his watch. Time for the elderly psychiatrist to watch his half-hour game show, and then make himself lunch. When he concentrated, Wilson could hear the TV upstairs in the doctor's living room.

At 12:35, the whistle of a teakettle announced the doctor's lunch preparations. Three minutes later, the kettle was still whistling furiously. Wilson abandoned his stakeout and hurried one flight up to see if anything was wrong.

When his knocking produced no response, Wilson walked into the unlocked apartment. The doctor lay on the kitchen floor. A fruit knife lay in his right hand. A bloody steak knife lay imbedded in his back.

Wilson did his own whistling. "Wow."

"Wow is correct, dear fellow."

The sergeant turned to find Sherman Holmes standing behind him in the doorway. "This murder just happened," Wilson gasped. "How do you do it? You're like a vulture."

"Thanks awfully," Sherman said and quickly perused the scene. The noisy teakettle sat on a low flame. On a cutting board were an open can of tuna and a sliced apple, its flesh already turned brown. The TV was on in the background. "Someone interrupted his lunch."

"That much seems clear," Wilson said. "There are two other tenants in this building who stay home during the day. Let's talk to them."

Sammy Cole, on the third floor, answered the door in his underwear. "I work nights," he said with a yawn. "I got home around 11 a.m., had a little breakfast, and went to bed." Sherman looked through to Cole's kitchen and saw a half-filled carafe sitting in the automatic coffee maker. "The floors are thick," Sammy added. "I didn't hear a thing."

Glenda Gould lived across the hall from Sammy and seemed unnerved by Dr. Weber's death. "He was my psychiatrist. I told him to get better security. With all the nut cases he treats, this sort of attack was inevitable." She twisted the ring on her finger, revealing a raw patch of skin underneath. "I'll need to find another doctor."

Wilson walked back down to the crime-scene apartment with Holmes. "Naturally I know who did it," Sherman said in his unique, infuriating way. "I just need to check one thing."

WHO IS SHERMAN'S SUSPECT?
WHAT WAS THE VITAL CLUE?

Solution on page 237.

A HALLOWEEN HOMICIDE

Sherman loved Halloween. It gave him a chance to dress up as Sherlock Holmes and still seem normal. The pudgy detective was in his usual costume, escorting a squadron of children down Elm Street, when he noticed a crowd gathering in front of old Miss Cleghorn's house. "She must be up to her usual," chortled Sherman. "Putting on some horrific mask and scaring the kids at the door."

Miss Cleghorn was indeed scaring the kids, but not intentionally. Inside the open door, Sherman could see her frail body lying in the entry hall, wearing a monster mask, her head surrounded by blood. A plastic bowl lay nearby, its contents of wrapped candy strewn everywhere.

Sergeant Wilson stood beside the body. He glanced over at the man with the calabash pipe and deer-stalker cap. "Is that a costume, Holmes? With you it's hard to tell."

"What happened, my respectable partner in crime?"

"It's an accident. It took us a while to reconstruct what happened." Wilson pointed up to where a strand of large pearls lay centered at the top of the steps. "She was upstairs when the first trick-or-treaters rang the bell. She put on the mask and grabbed the bowl. She must have slipped on the pearls and tumbled down the stairs."

Two cars pulled up at the curb, one behind the other. Sherman recognized Miss Cleghorn's niece and nephew, Emma and Bobby, as they got out of the cars and approached the front door, both dressed for a night out and seemingly unaware of the tragedy.

"Aunt Rita," Bobby gasped.

"Your aunt had an accident," Sergeant Wilson told them. "She's dead. The kids had been coming up to the door for half an hour or so and getting no answer. One of them finally looked through the window and saw her."

Bobby noticed the spilled candy and the mask. "What's she doing wearing a mask?"

"She was obviously doing her Halloween thing," Emma said.

"She promised she wouldn't this year. We were taking her out to dinner."

"Well, obviously she changed her mind," Emma said, shaking her head. "I don't know how many times I told her not to wear a mask on the stairs."

"When did you last see your aunt?" asked Sherman.

Bobby stared at the rather overage trick-or-treater. "Uh, I dropped by this morning. My daughter left her skateboard here. Aunt Rita made me coffee and we chatted."

Sergeant Wilson grabbed Sherman by the collar and dragged him aside. "Don't try to make this a murder. The neighbors say there were no visitors since this morning."

"Someone could have driven up the back alley and come in that way," argued Sherman. "Believe me, friend, this was murder."

WHY COULDN'T IT HAVE BEEN ACCIDENTAL?
WHOM DOES SHERMAN SUSPECT AND WHY?

Solution on page 237.

THE COMMERCIAL BREAK BREAK-IN

An inch of snow fell that evening, turning to a crusty sleet that hardened and made everything beautiful and treacherous. When the skies cleared, Sherman went for a stroll.

"What ho, Trent! A quiet night, eh?" Sherman waved to the uniformed guard hired to patrol the neighborhood.

"A little too quiet." Tom Trent was naturally suspicious and pessimistic, good traits for a neighborhood security guard. At the moment, he was scanning his flashlight beam across the suburban landscape. "Uh-oh." His light stopped on the side of the Warner family's home.

Sherman saw what he meant. The ladder that Bill Warner had used last fall to paint the house was now propped up against it, leading up to a second-story window. The flashlight beam scanned the rest of the house. Lights were on downstairs but not upstairs. The family had undoubtedly come home before the snowfall, since there were no footprints going up the walkway. But there were other footprints, a single set leading to the dry space under the eaves where the ladder was usually stored. The same prints led to where the ladder now stood, then retreated back to the sidewalk.

Trent checked out the ladder, stepping on the first rung and causing the wooden feet to crunch into the hardened snow. Without a word, the guard crossed to the front door, drew his revolver, and knocked. Sherman followed.

Amelia Warner answered the door. "Tom. Sherman. What's wrong?"

"Possible break-in," Trent replied, then asked a few questions. Amelia, Bill, and Frank, a visiting friend, had been home for about three hours. For the past hour, no one had gone upstairs. And no one had propped the ladder up against the house.

"Stay here," Trent ordered everyone. Then he tiptoed up the stairs and vanished around a corner. Two minutes later, he called out. "It's all clear. Come on up."

When Sherman, the Warners, and their houseguest entered the

master bedroom, they found the remains of a robbery. Drawers lay open; closets were in shambles. Bill and Amelia raced to check their valuables. Bill's wallet was gone. So were the rings and earrings from Amelia's jewelry box.

No one, it seems, had heard anything. "We were watching TV," Bill Warner said. "I went down to the basement during a commercial. I was looking for an old school yearbook to show Frank. I couldn't find it."

"I went to the kitchen for snacks and drinks," Amelia reported. "I think I went twice, during two commercial breaks."

"And I used the bathroom," said Frank. "Someone must have noticed the lights off upstairs and seen the ladder and just taken the opportunity. It wouldn't take long to grab the valuables. People always neglect to lock upstairs windows."

Amelia turned to Sherman. "You're always bragging about your great-great-grandfather. Why don't you put that genetic brilliance to a little use?"

WHO BURGLED THE BEDROOM?
HOW DID SHERMAN SOLVE THE CASE?

Solution on page 238.

AN ALARMING JEWEL HEIST

"Maybe now you'll stop bugging me," Zach Alban said as Sherman walked into his friend's shop. "See? I got that alarm system you recommended, wired straight to the police station."

"It's about time," Sherman replied. Alban Jewelers had just expanded its business and finally had some jewels worth stealing.

"Mr. Alban, I'm leaving now." Ricky Mayfield had finished clearing out the window displays, placing the felts of precious stones into their locked drawers for the night. The door buzzed as the young assistant raced out to catch his bus.

Melanie, Alban's second in command, was putting on her jacket and looking at the newly installed alarm panel. "Are you sure you don't want to give me the code, Zach? That way you won't always have to be here to open and close."

"Not right now. Maybe in a few days when I get more used to it."

"Whatever," Melanie said. A rumbling from the street announced the arrival of her boyfriend's motorcycle. "See you tomorrow." And she was quickly out the door, hopping onto the back of a Harley-Davidson.

Zach led the way into the back office, eager to show his friend the entire system. "Once I set the code, any broken window or open door will trigger the alarm. Twenty seconds, that's all the time I have to disarm it. Sam, why don't you go home, too?"

Sam Wells switched off the computer and wished his boss a

good night. Seconds later they heard the front door buzz, signaling the last employee's departure. "Want to help me close up?" Zach asked Sherman. "I don't want to make a mistake. After your first false alarm, they start charging you a fine."

Sherman and Zach followed the instructions to the letter, then went down the block to Gil's Tavern. When they left an hour later, Sherman noticed a police patrol car parked in front of Alban Jewelers.

"Break-in and burglary," an officer informed the devastated storeowner. "The back alley window was smashed. We responded within two minutes. But the alley was empty and the crooks were already gone."

Sherman was surprised by the thoroughness of the burglary. The jewel drawers had been chiseled open and stripped of their contents. The display cases had also been broken into and ransacked, glass shards littering the hardwood floor.

"So much for my brand new alarm system," Zach said almost accusingly.

"Not so fast," Sherman said. "If it weren't for the alarm system I wouldn't know who the burglar is."

WHO ROBBED THE SHOP?
HOW DO YOU KNOW?

Solution on page 239.

ALL IN THE FAMILY

Sergeant Wilson enjoyed an occasional breakfast with Sherman at the Baker Street Coffee Shop. What he didn't enjoy were the homicide calls that so often came right in the middle of the meal. He was just finishing his Belgian waffle with fruit when this morning's call took him to Gleason & Son Insurance, located on a lonely stretch of highway. As usual, Sherman tagged along.

A uniformed officer met them in the parking lot. "The victim is Gary Lovett," the officer told them. "A Gleason & Son employee. That's Neal Gleason and his sister, Patty Lovett. She's the victim's widow." He was pointing to an anxious-looking duo, both in their late twenties. "Mr. Gleason discovered the body at about 8:30 a.m."

Neal Gleason stepped forward. His statement sounded rehearsed. "When I pulled into the parking lot, I saw Gary's car. Gary is often here early, though he's always gone before noon. If Gary wasn't Patty's husband, Dad would've fired him long ago. The front door was open. Right inside the door I saw him, like that."

Wilson examined the body in the doorway. The man's head was a bloody mess, and it took the sergeant a while to realize that the rifle now bagged as evidence had been used as a blunt instrument, its wooden stock having been slammed into his head like a baseball bat. The body was cold and rigor mortis had already come and gone.

"That's my husband's rifle," volunteered the widow. "He kept it here at the office. Last night at home, Gary got this phone call. He said he had to go to the office and that I should just go to bed. I thought he might be going to see another woman. This morning when I woke up he was still gone. So I went to find him. I must have arrived here just a minute after my brother did."

"I think we should probably call Dad," Neal said.

That call wouldn't be necessary, for at that exact moment, George Gleason was pulling into the parking lot. The burly insurance broker eased himself out of his Cadillac and wordlessly took in the scene, the body, the bagged rifle, and his two children.

Patty ran up to him. "Someone murdered Gary," she moaned. "The police suspect us, Neal and me."

Gleason hugged his daughter, exchanged glances with his son, then turned to face Sergeant Wilson. "I killed him," he said softly and simply. "I met him here last night and shot him, right in the head. My kids had nothing to do with it."

As the uniform took Gleason's statement, Wilson stepped off to the side with Sherman. "You don't have to tell me," Wilson whispered. "I picked up on the clue, too."

"Perhaps, old man," Sherman said with a smile. "But did you pick up on the right clue?"

WHO KILLED GARY LOVETT?
WHAT CLUE POINTS TO THE KILLER?

Solution on page 239.

BLUE CARBUNCLE, THE SEQUEL

Once a year, on his birthday, Sherman Holmes threw a dinner party. The cream of Capital City's eccentrics would gather in his large, comfortable home, along with neighbors and other friends, to eat and drink and laugh.

At this year's celebration, after everyone else had left, Sherman and his three last guests sat over brandies in his living room, discussing the one inexhaustible topic, the Sherlock Holmes mysteries.

"What exactly is a carbuncle?" Dora Treat asked. Someone had brought up "The Adventure of the Blue Carbuncle," and the nurse practitioner was curious. "The only carbuncle I know is a skin infection, like a boil."

Buddy Johnson, a jeweler, chuckled. "It's a gemstone, a deep red garnet. Carbuncles are never blue. That was a figment of Conan Doyle's imagination."

Sherman puckered his round face into a frown. "But there is a blue carbuncle. Dr. Watson wouldn't lie about a thing like that."

"Yes, of course," Sam Pickering stammered. Their host seemed so rational in every other respect, it was easy to forget his fixation. "What Buddy meant was there are no other known blue carbuncles, just that one."

"Exactly," Sherman said. "That's why it was so expensive. Would you all like to see it?"

His guests were flabbergasted. "You mean you actually own the blue carbuncle?" asked Sam. "The one from the story?" The newspaper reporter had already done two articles about the unconventional millionaire and he could sense a third one in the making.

"The gem dealer assured me it's the real thing. Come into the library and I'll show you."

The room they walked into looked more like a junk room than a library, with first editions strewn on the chairs along with stacks of old papers and magazines. Sherman took three small boxes down from a shelf. He rummaged through the blue one, flipped through the red one, and finally found what he wanted in the green box.

"Here it is."

From among a pile of receipts and marbles, he pulled out a blue gem, about the size of a pea. Buddy Johnson pulled a jeweler's loop from his pocket and gave it a quick examination.

"It looks like a garnet," he said. "How amazing."

Each guest examined the strange stone, then returned it to their host.

While Dora excused herself to use the powder room, Sherman dropped the carbuncle into the red box and returned all three boxes to the shelf.

"You leave a priceless gem in a simple box?" Sam asked with a disapproving smirk. "With no security?"

Sherman puffed out his chest. "I am all the security it needs."

The guests stayed for another hour, then left at the same time. Normally, Sherman would have gone directly to bed. But some instinct led him back into the library.

He was shocked to see all three boxes lying open on the library table. Sherman went directly to the red box, then to the others. Sure enough, the carbuncle was gone.

He thought back. In the hour following the display of the jewel, each of his guests had wandered off, at least for a minute or two. It would have been chancy, but any one of them could have sneaked back into the library and stolen it.

Sherman was disappointed to think that one of his friends had robbed him. But his disappointment ran deeper. "Did the thief have such little regard for my detecting skills? How insulting! Would they have stolen from my great-great-grandfather and expected to get away with it?"

WHO STOLE THE BLUE CARBUNCLE?
WHAT GAVE THE THIEF AWAY?

Solution on page 240.

THE POKER FROM NOWHERE

Sherman Holmes and Sergeant Wilson stood side by side. They were staring at a bloody corpse sprawled face up in the living room of a suburban tract house.

Sherman spoke first. "A premeditated crime, what ho?"

Wilson frowned. "What makes you say that?"

"Choice of weapon." The round little man pointed at the fireplace poker. It had been used like a sword, stabbing its victim several times in the chest and stomach. "When we were walking up the drive, I didn't see any chimney."

Wilson looked around. "You're right. So, the killer brought the poker from another location, which indicates a planned murder. Very observant."

Holmes and Wilson had been in the midst of one of their occasional lunches when the call came in on the sergeant's cell phone. A mail carrier, making his rounds in a quiet neighborhood, had happened to glance through a living room window. He saw pretty much what they were seeing now, a large, elderly man who had died trying to fend off a brutal attack.

The responding patrolmen interviewed the next-door neighbor, a nearly deaf woman who claimed not to have heard or seen a thing.

"Harold Kipling." The sergeant was reading from the patrolman's notes. "A widower living alone. Three children, none of whom seemed fond of him. A life insurance policy was split among the kids, plus some savings. There had been fights about a nursing home and money."

"The children all live locally?" asked Sherman.

As if to answer the question, a patrolman eased open the door. "The victim's kids are here, Sarge. I told them he was dead. I hope that's okay."

The sergeant and his civilian partner walked out onto the lawn to face two middle-aged men and a woman. Wilson adopted his best corpse-side manner.

"Your father was murdered," he told them. "We don't know much more than that. The murder weapon was a fireplace poker."

"Fireplace poker? Dad doesn't have a fireplace," the older son said.

"We know that."

"So, what happened? Someone broke in with a poker and

stabbed him to death?"

"There were no signs of forced entry," Wilson explained. "Did your father get into many fights with people?"

The younger son found this amusing. "Just with us. He wanted to move into a nursing home. We didn't feel it was necessary."

"He wanted to go?" asked Wilson. This was certainly a switch.

"It's an expensive nursing home," volunteered the daughter. "He wanted to cash in his life insurance and use up his savings. It was a very selfish idea."

"I dropped over this morning," said Gary, the younger son. "Dad had already signed the papers. We argued about it, then I left. I called Jason and Jennifer."

"Right," said Jennifer. "Jason, Gary, and I decided we would come over as a group and try one last time. We got here just a few minutes ago."

"Can we see him?" Jason asked. There was a nervous timidity in his voice.

Sherman had been silent throughout the interview, but now he spoke up. "I think it would be fine for two of you to see the body. But one of you needs to answer a few more questions."

WHICH SUSPECT DOES SHERMAN WANT TO QUESTION?
WHAT CLUE MADE SHERMAN SUSPICIOUS?

Solution on page 241.

BUDDY BROWN

Sherman Holmes had been born and raised in Alabama and, despite his mania for Victorian England, had a deep, true affection for the American South. About once a year, usually on a warm spring weekend, he would gas up his antique Bentley and make the long pilgrimage back home.

Sherman himself was an orphan, but he had always kept in contact with his childhood neighbors, Buddy Brown and his clan. On one of his annual visits, the odd little detective found himself joining the Browns in every Alabamian's favorite pastime, a picnic.

The scene was a state park where the old southern family commandeered a picnic table. Buddy spread the tablecloth. Two of the grown children, Tiffany and Billy, unloaded the wicker baskets. The third, Julius, poured iced tea from a thermos, while their mother, Susan, unpacked the crystal salt and pepper shakers and handed out cloth napkins. Sherman added his own touch, a candelabra topped with citronella candles to keep away the bugs.

Although he saw the Browns just once a year, Sherman felt he knew them intimately. Julius was close to his own age, while Tiffany and Billy, the twins, were a good ten years younger. None were married, as if forming a family of their own might be some sort of affront to the domineering father who controlled their lives.

On the surface, the picnic resembled the dozen previous picnics he'd attended with the Browns. Billy flipped burgers on the grill. Julius kept everyone's glass full. Tiffany and Susan hovered over the proceedings, doling out seconds and thirds, while Buddy slathered butter on his corn, spilling half of it on his plate and wiping the other half from his mouth with a napkin.

But something was wrong. The jokes were strained, the affection too forced, and Sherman's sixth sense was kicking into gear. He tried to ignore it.

Buddy's heart attack came suddenly, near the end of the meal. The elderly man's fleshy face turned as white as his neatly trimmed mustache. His breathing grew heavy. Then he grasped his chest and collapsed backwards into the grass.

Sherman and Julius rushed to Buddy's side. The others gathered around, looking on helplessly as the two men did their best to revive the stricken patriarch.

"He's dead," Julius whispered.

Tiffany ran off to call an ambulance, but everyone knew it would be too late.

"He's had heart problems before," Billy said, then turned to comfort his mother. "This was the best way to go, Mom, surrounded by family and eating his favorite food."

Sherman had seen a few heart attacks in his time, and this certainly looked like one. He'd also seen more than a few poisonings.

Sherman glanced over at Buddy's place at the table. His glass was half full of iced tea. His plate held the remains of potato salad, coleslaw, and the uneaten sliver of a hamburger bun. A clean but rumpled napkin sat beside the plate, right next to the crystal salt shaker.

The detective's heart sank. Why did people try to get away with murder when he was around? It just didn't make sense.

WHO KILLED BUDDY?
WHAT CLUE GAVE THE KILLER AWAY?

Solution on page 242.

THE RING-STEALING RING

The teenagers sat around the bare table in the small, bare room. All three chewed and snapped their gum and looked sullen. Sherman Holmes and Zach Alban, the jewelry store owner, stood by helplessly, watching the two boys and the girl as all of them continued to wait for the police.

Zach led Sherman out into the hall where they could talk privately. "Are you sure they stole the ring?" he asked with a nervous twitch.

Sherman sighed. He almost wished he hadn't gotten involved. He had walked into Alban Jewelers that morning to have his pocket watch fixed. Almost immediately, he became suspicious of the girl and her two friends hovering over the ring counter. As a matter of habit, Sherman made a quick perusal of the display case.

While Zach Alban was examining Sherman's century-old time-piece, the three teenagers started heading for the exit. Sherman threw another quick glance toward the ring counter. The center-piece of the display, a sapphire and gold ring, was not where it had been just a minute before. It was gone.

For a short, heavyset person, Sherman could move surprisingly fast. "They're stealing a ring," he shouted as he raced to block the door.

The teenagers vehemently denied the theft and threatened a lawsuit if they weren't allowed to leave.

"I can't search them until the police arrive," Zach moaned. "Maybe it's all a mistake. Maybe I didn't put the ring out this morning. Or maybe someone stole it earlier and I didn't notice."

"The ring was there," Sherman assured him. "One of them stole it."

Red and white lights flashed through the windows as a police cruiser pulled into the handicap parking space. Two officers entered, were briefed on the situation, and were led into the small back room.

The female officer searched the girl, Hanna Bright, while the male officer frisked both Josh Ingram and Timmy Bright, Hanna's brother. Their possessions were searched as well. A quick visual inspection of the room showed no place where the ring could have been hidden.

Zach Alban was profuse with apologies to everyone except Sherman. When the teens complained of being hungry, Zach ran out to the fast-food restaurant next door and returned a few minutes later with mounds of food. Hanna and Josh removed the wads of gum from their mouths before sinking into the hot double cheeseburgers.

"We came in to buy a present for Josh's mom." Food was sticking to Hanna's braces as she spoke. "Is this how you treat

customers? We're telling everyone not to shop here."

"Maybe we'll organize a boycott," Josh added. "How would you like a picket line, Mr. Alban?"

Sherman took Zach aside. "I wasn't wrong," he insisted. "One of those kids took the ring. And what's more, I can prove it."

WHO STOLE THE RING?
WHERE IS THE RING NOW?

Solution on page 243.

MRS. KRENSHAW'S SPARE KEY

"I hate to bother you, Mr. Holmes."

Sherman's neighbor, Mrs. Krenshaw, led him across the street from his house to hers, a tidy Victorian gem set in the pristine white of a recent snowfall. The elderly widow was remarkably self-sufficient and walked with a strong, confident gait.

"I know I ought to go to the police," she said in a fluttering voice. "But Hank and Edgar are both such good friends. If you could find some way of getting my vase back without calling in the authorities..." She pressed her hand into his. "You're so very clever about these things."

Sherman blushed and cleared his throat. "Tell me about the vase, Mrs. Krenshaw."

She spoke eagerly. "You know that TV program, *America's Treasures*, the one where people bring in antiques and the experts tell where they came from and how much they're worth. Well, I had this old vase handed down to me by my mother. I took it over to the Armory yesterday, where they were filming the show. An expert appraised it at $20,000. It was all very exciting, being on TV and having such a rarity."

"And you think either Hank or Edgar broke into your house and stole it?"

"I don't know what else to think. Look."

Sherman looked. In the middle of the lawn sat a flowerpot on top of a stump. A single set of footprints crossed the snow-covered lawn to the stump then crossed away again toward the front door. Mrs. Krenshaw trampled through the snow to the stump.

"The house was unlocked when I got home from shopping a few minutes ago. I never leave it unlocked. Sure enough, the antique vase was gone. Then I saw these footprints out here. I came right over to you." She lifted the flowerpot and pointed to a

key hidden beneath it. "I know it's stupid to leave a key out here like this, but everybody does it."

"Both Edgar and Hank know where you keep your spare key?"

"Yes. And they knew about the vase. I just had to tell them my wonderful news."

Once inside the house, Sherman telephoned Hank, Lyda Krenshaw's next-door neighbor, and Edgar, a gentleman friend who lived two blocks away. Hank was the first to arrive.

"I've been home all morning," Hank explained. He was a young, slight bachelor and didn't seem outraged to be considered a suspect. "I was paying bills at my desk. It's got a view of the street and I didn't notice any cars stopping or people walking by. Of course, I wasn't staring out the window every second." Sherman checked the man's shoes. They were wet from the snow, but his trouser legs appeared dry.

Edgar rang the bell a few minutes later. He seemed more annoyed by Sherman's inquiries. "I took my dog for a walk this morning. I passed by this block, but I didn't see anyone. And I certainly didn't go into Lyda's house."

Sherman left the men and joined Mrs. Krenshaw in the kitchen. "I'm not sure I can help you," he admitted. "Was the vase insured?"

She thought for a moment. "I suppose it's covered by my home-owner's policy. Does this mean you don't know who took it?"

"Oh, I know who took it. I just don't think you'll like the answer."

WHO STOLE THE VASE?
WHAT CLUE GAVE THE THIEF AWAY?

Solution on page 243.

CHECK THE BRAKES

It was a balmy, late summer evening. Sergeant Wilson examined the mangled body in the driver's seat, exchanging a few words with his forensics crew. When he finally trudged up the side of the ravine to the break in the railing, he was only slightly surprised to find Sherman Holmes pulling his antique Bentley into the roadside turnout.

"Well, that clinches it," Wilson muttered. "If Sherman shows up on the scene, it's got to be murder. Good evening, Mr. Holmes."

"Evening, my good Wilson." Sherman scanned the broken railing and the winding, downhill road leading to it. "No tire marks. May we assume that the driver's brakes malfunctioned?"

"Brake lines were neatly cut. The victim is one Milton Graves. His driver's license says he lives up the hill. Want to join me while I break the news to his next of kin?"

The men hopped into a police cruiser and hopped out again in front of a comfortable mountain retreat. The thirtyish, attractive woman answering the door identified herself as Dominique Black, the niece and personal lawyer of the deceased.

Dominique seemed stunned by the tragic news and asked the sergeant and his companion to step inside. The first thing Sherman noticed was a balloon bouquet nestled high in the oaken rafters.

"A birthday party?" he inquired.

"For Uncle Milton," she answered. "My cousins and I came over for a little celebration. Afterwards, Uncle Milton drove off to pick up another cousin at the airport. We were expecting them back any moment. And now you say he's dead?"

"Yes, ma'am. Probably just minutes after leaving the house." Wilson didn't mention the brake lines.

The other inhabitants wandered into the entry hall and were informed of the news. The cousins, Tyrone and Chuck Graves, seemed just as stunned as Dominique, while the housekeeper, Mrs. Watts, reacted with a chilly frown.

"Do you know anyone who might have wanted your uncle dead?"

"I can think of three," Mrs. Watts answered. "During dessert, Mr. Graves made an announcement. He had just changed his will. Instead of leaving his money to charity, he had divided his estate evenly among his nieces and nephews."

"That's right," Tyrone admitted. "It came as a complete shock."

"What a tragic coincidence!" Chuck could barely repress a grin.

"Exactly," agreed Sherman. "What did you all do after dinner?"

Chuck, a Wall Street broker, answered first. "I was overwhelmed by the news. I telephoned my wife as soon as we left the table. I was still on the phone when Uncle Milton drove off."

Tyrone, a pediatric surgeon, had a similar, equally provable alibi. "I was on my cell phone, talking to the hospital. I imagine the phone company can verify the time."

"And I was with Uncle Milton," Dominique said, "taping a video birthday greeting for the company offices. Mrs. Watts was working the camera."

Mrs. Watts nodded. "Why do you need to know this, officer?"

"For our report," Wilson replied, then took Sherman aside. He looked disappointed. "If their stories check out, Sherman, we're stumped. None of them had a chance to get to the garage and tamper with the brakes."

"But someone did tamper with the brakes," Sherman said. "And I think I know who."

WHO CUT THE BRAKE LINES?
HOW DID SHERMAN KNOW?

Solution on page 244.

DEATH OF A SWINGER

"We had an abandoned quarry like this back home." Despite the tragic scene, Sherman couldn't repress a smile. "The local swimming hole. I remember being a kid and swinging on a rope, Tarzan-style, just like this poor fellow.'

His wistful tone contrasted sharply with the bloody, broken body just in front of him. The deceased was a youth of about twenty, wearing swim trunks and lying on a granite slab a dozen feet from the edge of a deep, clear pool. Wreathing the body was a thirty-foot length of rope.

Sergeant Wilson lifted the corpse to reveal the rope's freshly severed end. "See? The rope was cut halfway through, then torn the rest of the way." He held the body up as Sherman inspected the rope, then settled the body back down on top of it. "This was murder."

Both men turned and looked up the sheer rock face. Sixty feet above them was the cliff on which Bobby Fixx had stood. Even from here, Sherman could see the other end of the rope, tied to the branch of a towering pine. The ten-foot section swayed gently in the summer breeze.

"Looks pretty obvious," Wilson said. "Our Mr. Fixx swings out on the rope, just like he's done a hundred times before. Only this time, someone's cut through it. Instead of swinging into the water,

he falls straight down, taking this useless piece of rope with him."

"Isn't this area private property?" asked Sherman.

"Yep," said Wilson. "Owned by Midlands Granite. Fixx and his college buddies rent an off-campus house just over the ridge. Let's go pay them a visit."

They found the three college juniors sitting in stunned silence on the porch of a tattered cabin. Sergeant Wilson checked his notes. "Thad Killian? You actually saw it happen?"

"Yeah." The short blond boy on the porch swing nodded his head. "I was hiking along the ridge, a couple hundred yards from the cliff. I saw Bobby. He grabbed the rope and took a running start. As soon as he cleared the edge, the rope broke. He screamed and then there was this thud instead of a splash. I came right back here and called 911."

"I heard the scream, too," said a tall, burly redhead. "I'm Rick Dawson. I was walking on the road, by the barbed-wire fence. I figured the scream must have come from the swimming quarry. That's the only reason anyone goes there. I hopped the fence and found his body a few minutes later. I didn't touch anything."

"Forensics will know if you did," the sergeant said curtly. He approached the third student. "You must be Julio Mendez."

"Right," answered the last roommate. "I was supposed to go swimming with Bobby today, but I fell asleep. Thad woke me after he called 911." He shivered. "I used that rope swing as much as Bobby. It could have been me dying like that."

Wilson took his friend aside. "This could be a hard one, Sherman. We don't even know if Fixx was the intended target. Whoever sawed through that rope . . . "

"Whoever sawed through that rope is right here on this porch. I don't know what the motive was, but one of Fixx's roommates is definitely lying."

WHO KILLED BOBBY FIXX?
WHAT GAVE THE KILLER AWAY?

Solution on page 245.

MATCH WITS
WITH
THOMAS P. STANWICK

MEET YOUR COLLEAGUE

Meet Thomas P. Stanwick, a lean and lanky young man, standing six feet two inches tall. His long, thin face is complemented by a full head of brown hair and a droopy mustache. Though not husky in build, he is surprisingly strong and enjoys ruggedly good health.

He is undeniably well educated; he graduated with high honors from Dartmouth College as a philosophy major and studied logic and history at Cambridge University. He now lives alone (with a pet Labrador) in a bungalow in the New England town of Baskerville, not far from the city of Royston. His house is filled with books, chess sets, maps, and charts.

He earns a living as a freelance editor of textbooks on geometry and American history. Stanwick is good-humored and amiable, but first and foremost, he is a logician, particularly skilled in traditional formal deduction. His personal tastes are simple and he has several British habits—he prefers tea to coffee, for example, and smokes a pipe.

He takes long travel vacations in the summertime and often visits the Earl of Stanwyck, a distant relative, at the earl's East Anglian estate or at his country estate in Scotland.

When he has a hand in investigating and solving crimes, it is usually through his friendship with Inspector Matt Walker, a promising detective on the Royston police force. Join them as they play chess together at the chess club on Thursday evenings, and accompany Stanwick when he drops by police headquarters.

THE CASE OF
THE WELLS FARGO MONEY

The daring theft of half a million dollars from a Wells Fargo armored truck captured the imagination of the entire Royston area. As the *Royston Gazette* excitedly summarized it, the truck had just been loaded with cash from the First National Bank on the afternoon of June 4 when two or three men appeared, overpowered the guards, piled the money into a pickup truck, and disappeared—all in less than five minutes.

The investigation was placed in the hands of Inspector Matthew Walker. His skillful inquiries led the police to three men who often worked together and were suspected of several lesser robberies.

Some 10 miles from the city, in the little town of Baskerville, Thomas P. Stanwick, the amateur logician, pushed aside a postal chess analysis and admitted the inspector to his bungalow.

"I'm delighted to see you, Matt," said Stanwick as they seated themselves in the living room. "I hear you've been doing fine work on this Wells Fargo case."

"Thanks, Tom." Walker smiled wearily. "All the public attention has put a lot of pressure on us to solve it and, if possible, recover the money."

"I've also heard you have some suspects under surveillance."

"That's right. This is strictly confidential, of course." Walker leaned forward in his armchair. "We have conclusive evidence that Charles Acker, Bull Barrington, and Adam Crowley organized the job, and at least two of them actually carried it out. We've been monitoring their communications, hoping to get more information. The money has been hidden, and not all three of them know where it is. It would aid us enormously to find out who knows its location.

"To complicate matters, at least one of them communicates by a 'lying code', in which everything he says is false. The others speak truthfully. We don't know which, or how many of them, are using the lying code."

Stanwick idly twisted the tip of his mustache and chuckled.

"Quite a problem. Can I help?"

"I hope so." Walker flipped open his notebook. "These are the only helpful statements we've been able to intercept that might tell us who's lying and who knows where the money is:

Acker: Barrington is using the lying code, and I know where the money is.

Barrington: Acker was out of town at the time of the robbery.

Crowley: Acker was in town at the time of the robbery if and only if he knows where the money is.

Barrington: I don't use the lying code.

Acker: Either I was in town at the time of the robbery or Crowley does not use the lying code.

Crowley: Not all of us use the lying code. I don't know where the money is.

"As you can see, it's a bit of a tangle," Walker concluded.

Stanwick took and studied the notebook for a few minutes, and then handed it back.

"My dinner's almost ready," he said, standing up. "Pot roast, potatoes, and peas. Since you'll be working late anyway, I hope you can stay long enough to join me. In the meantime, I'll be glad to tell you who is lying, and at least one man who knows where the money is."

WHO IS LYING? WHO KNOWS WHERE THE MONEY IS?

Solution on page 247.

A SLAYING IN THE NORTH END

"Well, Matt, what big-city crimes are testing the skills and trying the patience of Royston's finest this week?"

Thomas P. Stanwick, the amateur logician, grinned at Inspector Walker as he dropped into the visitor's chair of the inspector's chronically cluttered office. Stretching his long legs toward the desk, he fumbled for his pipe.

Walker looked up wearily.

"Good to see you, Tom. I thought you were all tied up with that geometry textbook revision."

"That should be finished by Friday," replied Stanwick, lighting his briar. "By next Wednesday, I'll be off to London and Cambridge

for two weeks of loitering, puttering in musty bookshops, and reminiscing about student days. What's up, though? You look frazzled."

"I sure am." Walker pawed through a pile of papers on his desk and pulled out four. "These are my notes on the Minot Street shooting. I've been up all night compiling them. There are still several gangs fighting up there in the North End. Les Chaven, the leader of the Blackhawks, was shot and killed last Friday afternoon by a member of the Leopards, apparently in a turf fight over Minot Street."

"So both gangs love Minot, eh?" said Stanwick.

Walker winced. "The members of the Leopard gang," the inspector continued, "are Al Foster, Bruce Diskin, Charlie Jensen, Damon O'Keefe, and Eddie Lyons. Their gang is pretty new, so we don't know yet which is the leader. Nor do we know which is the killer. So far, all I've been able to dig up are these facts:

"1. The killer and the leader had a fierce argument about whether to kill Chaven before deciding to go ahead with it.

"2. Jensen works the evening shift as a machinist in the local plant on weeknights and is thinking of working at his brother's gym-bag factory in San Francisco.

"3. The leader's wife is a teller at the Second National Bank. Foster, an only child, works part-time as a janitor there.

"4. The leader and Diskin play poker every Tuesday night at eight over Hiller's Saloon. Foster picks them up there after midnight and drives them home.

"5. Jensen is married to the killer's sister, who was once engaged to O'Keefe.

"6. O'Keefe, a bachelor, is the best lockpick of the five."

Stanwick, fingering the tip of his mustache, quietly glanced over Walker's notes and then handed them back. An amused twinkle lit his eye as he watched Walker give a gaping yawn.

"What you need," he said, "is a little more sleep. If you weren't so tired, I'm sure you'd see that there's easily enough information here to deduce the identities of both the leader and the killer."

WHO IS THE LEADER?
WHO IS THE KILLER?

Solution on page 247.

BAD DAY FOR BERNIDI

During a midday visit to the city of Royston, Thomas P. Stanwick, the amateur logician, noticed several police cars at the entrance of Bernidi's, a small downtown jewelry store. Toying with the tip of his mustache in thoughtful curiosity, he approached and eased his way through a knot of onlookers. His friend Inspector Matt Walker was inside, and he signaled to the policeman at the door to let Stanwick in.

"Hello, Tom," exclaimed Walker in mild surprise. "What brings you here?"

"I was just passing by," replied Stanwick. He glanced around the cool, dark interior of the narrow room. "What happened?"

"I was just about to ask Mr. Bernidi to repeat his story to me."

The two turned to the small, white-haired owner, who was leaning against one of the two display counters that ran the length of both sides of the room. His face was streaked with dust, and he looked exhausted.

"I had just stepped into the back," he said, "when I hear the bell on the front door ring. I come out, and there's this guy, very well dressed, looking around and coming toward me and the register. 'Can I help you?' I say, and he smiles and pulls a gun halfway out of his jacket pocket. A little piece, but I can see it's real. Then he puts it back, but keeps his hand in there. There's nobody else around, so what can I do?

"Anyway, he makes me open the register, but I just made a deposit, so there's only a few bucks. He doesn't get mad, but takes a piece of clothesline out of another pocket, ties my hands behind my back, and makes me lie down on my stomach behind the side counter here, with my face to the wall.

"It was tight; you can see there's not much room back there. Then I hear him opening the wood panels—these here, the lower half of the counter—but he finds nothing. I only keep supplies down there. Then he steps across to the opposite counter, pulls out a little burlap sack, smashes the glass, scoops some rings into the sack, and runs out. I get up, see the broken glass, and yell for a cop."

"What did the man look like?" asked Walker.

"Like I told the officer—big, burly guy, clean-shaven, dark hair."

"Don't you have your display glass wired to an alarm?" inquired Stanwick.

"Never got around to it. It's insured, anyway."

"Well, thank you, Mr. Bernidi," said Walker, closing his notebook. "We'll check around and let you know when we make an arrest."

"I think you can make an arrest right now," said Stanwick quietly.

WHOM DOES STANWICK SUSPECT, AND WHY?

Solution on page 248.

AN UNACCOUNTABLE DEATH

On this rainy Tuesday, as on many other Tuesdays around noon, Thomas P. Stanwick, the amateur logician, called on his friend Inspector Matt Walker in the inspector's tiny, cluttered office in Royston. Walker usually had a case or two on hand that he knew would pique the interest and exercise the particular talents of his friend. This day was no exception.

"We've got a shooting death on our hands, Tom," said Walker, leaning back in his chair. "Herb Lombard, the manager of a small accounting firm in the Cummins Building, was found dead at his desk late yesterday afternoon. He may have shot himself, but we're not sure."

Stanwick idly fingered the tip of his mustache.

"Who discovered the body?" he asked.

"A client of his named John Morey, who works in another office down the hall. Lombard was working on some late personal tax returns for him. Morey says he was leaving work yesterday, shortly after five, when he passed the door of Lombard's firm and decided to see if Lombard was in. The clerks had already left the outer office, but light was shining from under the door of Lombard's inner office.

"Morey knocked, opened the door, and found Lombard slumped over his desk in a puddle of blood with a revolver in his hand. Morey was so scared that, without touching anything in the room, he ran down to a pay phone in the lobby and called headquarters.

"I arrived a few minutes later and accompanied him back to Lombard's inner office. Snapping on the light, I found everything just as Morey had described. Lombard had been dead for less than an hour, and had a bullet wound in his head. The revolver had been fired once."

Stanwick shifted slightly in his chair.

"Poor devil," he remarked. "Did Morey find the door to the outer office open?"

"No, but it had been left unlocked," replied Walker.

"I see." Stanwick looked grim. "You'd better arrest Morey at once, Matt. He's lying about this affair!"

WHY DOES STANWICK SUSPECT MOREY?

Solution on page 248.

THE CASE OF THE PURLOINED PAINTING

There were times, thought Thomas P. Stanwick, when you could never count on having a friendly conversation without an interruption. Especially if your friend was a police inspector and you were visiting his office when a robbery call came in.

The amateur logician and Inspector Walker pulled up in front of a large brick house in a wealthy neighborhood in Royston and were quickly shown into the living room. A valuable painting had been stolen from the wall. The thief had apparently broken the glass in a nearby patio door, let himself in, and left by the same route. An obviously shaken maid was sitting in a large armchair when Stanwick and Walker entered.

"She discovered the theft and called it in, sir," a uniformed officer told Walker. "The couple who live here are out of town this week."

"What happened?" Walker asked the maid.

"I didn't hear a thing," she replied. "I had been working in the kitchen and was on my way to my room. When I passed the living room, I noticed that the painting was gone and that the glass in the patio door was broken. I called the police right away."

Stanwick carefully opened the patio door and walked out onto the concrete patio, stepping gingerly around the long shards of broken glass there as well as around any possible footmarks. He observed faint smudges of mud under the glass.

"How long had the painting hung in here?" he asked as he came back in.

"About two years, I guess," answered the maid.

Stanwick sat down in a comfortable arm-chair, crossed his legs, and turned to Walker.

"Well, Matt," he said, "I think you may want to ask this lady some more questions. This job involved inside help!"

WHY IS STANWICK
SURE THAT INSIDE
HELP WAS INVOLVED?

*Solution
on page 248.*

THE WEEK OF THE QUEEN ANNE FESTIVAL

Ah, to be in England, now that summer's here, thought Thomas P. Stanwick as he descended to the pub for breakfast. He was beginning a two-month vacation in England with a week's stay at the Grey Boar Inn, a few miles outside Knordwyn.

The amateur logician had first visited Knordwyn, a tiny village in Northumbria, a year earlier, and had become very fond of it and greatly intrigued by its peculiarities. Chief among these was that about half the villagers always told the truth, and the rest always lied. Stanwick thus found his conversations there wonderful challenges for his powers of deduction.

It was a beautiful Monday morning, and Stanwick gathered his thoughts over a hearty breakfast of eggs, bacon, toast, and tea. He knew that this was the week of the Queen Anne Festival, held annually in Knordwyn since Queen Anne stopped overnight in the village on her way to visit Scotland in 1702. People gathered on festival days from many surrounding towns to enjoy dancing, balladeering, cooking, racing, and other activities.

The trouble was that the festival date and the number of festival days varied from year to year, and Stanwick wasn't sure which days this year were the festival days. He knew that today was not a festival day, and that the festival would be over before Saturday. At least one, and possibly more, of the intervening days would be festival days, and he wanted to know precisely which.

Finishing his breakfast, Stanwick lit his pipe, leaned back in his chair, and idly fingered a tip of his brown mustache as he looked slowly around the room. The other tables were empty except for one by a large window. Around that table were gathered three grizzled villagers, all cronies of the innkeeper, nursing early mugs of ale. Stanwick had seen them before and knew that their names were Chiswick, Green, and Hunter, but he didn't know which were liars and which were truth-tellers. Well, he thought, perhaps today he would find out.

Stanwick arose and strolled over to their table.

"Good morning, gentlemen," he said cheerfully. "I beg your pardon, but could you please tell me which days this week are festival days? Also, if you'll excuse my asking, which of you are liars?"

The three villagers glanced at each other silently for a moment. Chiswick was the first to speak.

"We are all liars," said he, "and Friday is a festival day."

"He speaks the truth," Green said. "Also, Tuesday is a festival day."

Hunter took a gulp from his mug.

"If Chiswick is lying," he said as he set it down, "then Green is telling the truth. Also, Wednesday is a festival day."

"Thank you, gentlemen," said Stanwick, who turned and walked off with a delighted smile. He now knew which of the three were liars and which days that week were festival days.

WHO IS LYING?

WHICH DAYS ARE FESTIVAL DAYS?

Solution on page 249.

DEATH OF A CON MAN

Thomas P. Stanwick was engrossed in revising some notes at his desk late one spring afternoon when the doorbell rang. He opened the door and found Inspector Walker standing on the step.

"Matt! Come in," Stanwick exclaimed, stepping aside. "It's nice of you to drop by on your way back to Royston."

Walker looked surprised.

"How did you know which direction I came from?" he asked. "I parked in the driveway, not on the street."

"Quite so, but I observe that the small mud patch by the driveway entrance on the side toward Royston is undisturbed. Had you come from Royston, you could hardly have avoided at least grazing it as you turned in."

Walker laughed as they settled themselves into a pair of comfortable armchairs in the living room.

"Never expect to keep secrets when you visit a logician," he said. "I'm on my way back from Richford, where I've been following up some leads on the Edmunds murder last week."

"Edmunds? Isn't he the con man who was shot in a shipping warehouse?" asked Stanwick as he relit his pipe.

"That's right. We've arrested four members of a gang he recently fleeced: Cannon, Cochran, Carruthers, and Carpenter. We know one of them is the killer. Our polygraph showed that each made one true statement and one false statement this morning under interrogation, but we couldn't determine which was which."

Stanwick leaned forward eagerly. "Do you have a copy of the statements?"

Walker smiled, reached into his coat pocket, and pulled out a folded document.

"I thought you might find them interesting," he said as he handed the paper across. "If you can make any use of them, I'd be glad to hear your conclusions."

Stanwick unfolded the paper, leaned back, and read:

Cannon: I did not kill Edmunds. Carpenter is the killer.

Cochran: I did not kill Edmunds. Cannon is lying when he says Carpenter is the killer.

Carruthers: I did not kill Edmunds. Either Cannon is the killer or none of us is.

Carpenter: I did not kill Edmunds. If Carruthers did not kill Edmunds, then Cannon did.

"At least they were all consistent with their denials," Stanwick said with a laugh. "However, a little deduction is enough to clear up the matter. The killer is . . . "

WHO IS THE KILLER?

Solution on page 249.

THE CASE OF THE
EDGEMORE STREET SHOOTING

"Thanks for coming over, Tom," said Inspector Matt Walker as Thomas P. Stanwick, the amateur logician, strolled into the inspector's office at Royston Police headquarters.

"Glad to," Stanwick replied as he flopped into a chair. "You said you were going to interrogate a suspect in that recent street shooting."

"That's right." Walker lit a cheap cigar. "As you may already know, Bruce Walder, a local businessman in his mid-fifties, was walking along Edgemore Street about dusk two days ago. Someone approached him, shot him in the chest, and ran off. We suspect that the shooter wanted to rob him, and shot him when Walder started to resist.

"We haven't located anyone who actually saw the crime, but several locals were able to describe a man they saw lounging in the street shortly before it took place.

Their descriptions matched that of Victor Kravitz, a small-time mugger known to frequent the area. We picked up Kravitz just a few hours ago. Let's hear what he has to say."

They went to a nearby interrogation room. Kravitz, a small, nervous man with thinning blond hair, sat beside his lawyer and chain-smoked. Two detectives leaned against the wall while Walker and Stanwick sat down at the table.

"You've got it all wrong," cried Kravitz. "I didn't shoot Walder. I was on the street earlier, sure, but just hanging around. When I saw some guy come out of an alley, come up behind the stiff, and shoot him, I ran. I didn't want no trouble."

"You saw the crime committed?" asked Walker.

"Yeah. Yeah."

"Why didn't you report it?" asked one of the other detectives.

Kravitz laughed nervously. "Sure. Like you guys were about to believe me."

"Can you describe the man?" Walker inquired.

"Sure, sure. Middle-aged guy, tall, red mustache. Wore a big gray overcoat and a hat. Walder never even saw him."

"Where did you run to?"

"My girlfriend's place. You can ask her."

Stanwick, who had been slouching back in his chair, cleared his throat and slowly sat up.

"I for one have heard enough, Matt," he said to Walker. "This man is obviously lying."

HOW DOES STANWICK KNOW THAT KRAVITZ IS LYING?

Solution on page 250.

DEATH COMES TO THE COLONEL

Thomas P. Stanwick, the amateur logician, and Inspector Matthew Walker of the Royston Police strode into the richly carpeted study of Jeremy Huddleston. It was a chilly Tuesday in late fall, and Stanwick had been chatting in Walker's office when word came in of Huddleston's sudden death. Poisoning was suspected.

Huddleston, a retired army colonel in his seventies, lay behind his desk in the middle of the room, partly covered by his overturned chair. His sightless eyes stared at the ceiling as a fire crackled in the large brick hearth behind the desk. Near the hearth, a young, balding man sat wearily in an armchair. Walker approached him.

"Mr. Huddleston?" he asked. "Mr. George Huddleston?"

The young man nodded.

"The colonel's grandnephew, aren't you?"

"Yes."

"Please tell us what happened."

Huddleston looked up nervously and wet his lips. "I came into the study about ten this morning to say good morning to Uncle Jeremy. He was working at his desk and seemed to be in cheerful spirits. He asked me to pour him another cup of coffee from the sideboard, so I did. He drank about half of it, and then suddenly put his cup down and said, 'Before I forget, I must call Phillips to

fix the leak in the basement pipes.'"

"Roy Phillips, the local plumber?" Walker cut in.

"That's right." Huddleston continued. "He had just started to dial his private phone when he uttered a sharp cry, clutched suddenly at his throat, and fell over onto the floor. I was horrified and rushed over to him, but could see at once that he was dead.

"Hurrying out to the hall, I locked the study door and called to his housekeeper, Mrs. Stowe, who phoned the doctor and the police. I kept the study door locked until you arrived."

A medical assistant touched Walker on the shoulder.

"Excuse me, sir," he said. "The drops we extracted from the coffee cup show definite traces of cyanide."

Walker nodded. Stanwick lit his pipe and looked slowly around the room. His gaze rested in turn on the cheery fire warming the room of death, on the half-empty coffee cup resting neatly in its saucer, and on the West Point ring adorning the victim's finger.

"Do you live here, Mr. Huddleston?" Stanwick asked, suddenly turning to the nephew.

"No," replied Huddleston. "I live in California, where I work for an architecural firm. I was here only for the week, to visit Uncle Jeremy and see the East Coast again."

The phone on the colonel's desk rang. Walker answered it and bluntly told the caller, an old friend of the colonel's nephew, that the colonel was dead and a police investigation was in progress. After hanging up, he faced George Huddleston again.

"What more can you tell us, Mr. Huddleston?" he asked.

"Nothing," replied Huddleston listlessly.

"On the contrary," said Stanwick sharply, "I think Mr. Huddleston could help by telling us the truth."

HOW DOES STANWICK KNOW THAT HUDDLESTON IS LYING?

Solution on page 250.

STANWICK FINDS THE MAGIC WORDS

The small downtown section of Baskerville was unusually busy that Saturday morning. After browsing through several other stores, Thomas P. Stanwick wandered into the Baskerville Bookshop, a crowded, bright little store displaying books, greeting cards and, in a far corner, toys. He was looking for a birthday present for the younger son of his friend Inspector Matt Walker. Tim Walker was about to turn six.

Weaving his way through knots of other customers, Stanwick made his way to the toy corner. There he spotted a toy he knew Tim would love: a bright red fire truck. Scooping it up, Stanwick started for the checkout counter and then stopped with a sudden realization. He had accidentally left his wallet at home.

With a sigh of annoyance, Stanwick turned to put the truck back. As he did, he saw a sign near a collection of puzzle books:

SAY THE MAGIC WORDS!

How sharp are your puzzle skills? Tell us the logical conclusion of the following statements and win the book or toy of your choice!

1. All friends of winged armadillos wear striped ties.
2. Only those who eat pickled harmonicas can enter a chocolate courtroom.
3. Members of the Diagonal Club drink martinis only at four.
4. All who eat pickled harmonicas are friends of winged armadillos.

5. Only those green elephants who are members of the Diagonal Club can wear striped ties.

6. All green elephants drink martinis at five.

Stanwick's eyes sparkled. For a few moments, he stood stock still, staring at the sign and fingering the tip of his mustache. Then, with a gesture of triumph, he swung the truck back under his arm, strode to the checkout counter, and won the truck for Tim by saying the magic words.

WHAT ARE THE MAGIC WORDS?

Solution on page 251.

INSPECTOR WALKER FEELS THE HEAT

"Hello, Tom? Matt here. Have you got a few minutes to spare this afternoon? We're really up against it here, and I could use some advice. Mind if I come right over? Thanks."

As Thomas P. Stanwick hung up the phone, he reflected that his friend Inspector Walker, who had just called from police headquarters, sounded unusually tense and anxious. A few prominent citizens of the city of Royston had been assaulted recently, and Stanwick wondered if one of those cases might be troubling Walker.

Within half an hour, the inspector had driven out from Royston and arrived at Stanwick's bungalow in Baskerville. The amateur logician promptly ushered him into the living room, where they sat down.

"You look pretty harried, Matt," observed Stanwick as he filled his pipe. "What's up?"

"It's the attack on the deputy mayor two nights ago," Walker replied.

"Ah, yes. I remember reading something about it in the paper. Beaten and robbed as he walked home after

attending a late neighborhood committee meeting, I think."

"That's right. He wasn't very badly hurt, but is still in the hospital. The night was so dark, and the attack so sudden, that he isn't sure whether he was attacked by one man or several. The mayor has ordered an all-out investigation, and has really turned on the pressure."

Stanwick grinned faintly. "I can imagine."

"Our search," continued Walker, "has narrowed down to five men. One is Robert Ellis, a small-time mugger. The other four are a gang of ruffians from the north end of the city. Their names are Al Chase, Archie Heath, Dick Mullaney, and Bull Decker. At least one of the five is guilty."

"What can you tell me about them?"

Walker took out his notebook.

"We've spent the last two days," he said, "checking the activities of the gang members that night. So far, we've learned only enough to be sure of the following:

"1. If Chase is guilty and Heath is innocent, then Decker is guilty.

"2. If Chase is innocent, then Mullaney is innocent.

"3. If Heath is guilty, then Mullaney is guilty.

"4. Chase and Heath are not both guilty.

"5. Unless Heath is guilty, Decker is innocent.

"That's all of it, Tom. Not many hard facts, I'm afraid. The heat is really on, though, so if you can deduce anything more from what we have, I'll be very grateful."

Stanwick accepted the notebook and studied its scribbled entries with complete absorption. Walker, still agitated and restless, got up and paced the floor.

A few moments later, Stanwick closed the notebook and looked up with a smile.

"Well, Matt," he said cheerfully, "it's about time you relaxed. You've given me enough to determine who is guilty and who is innocent in this matter."

WHO ASSAULTED THE DEPUTY MAYOR?

Solution on page 251.

STANWICK VISITS SCOTLAND YARD

"Stanwick, my dear fellow," exclaimed Bodwin, "you couldn't possibly have chosen a better moment to come to London."

"London in April hasn't quite the reputation of the French capital," replied Thomas P. Stanwick with a grin as he sat down. "Still, I'm always glad to be back."

The amateur logician had stopped at Scotland Yard to visit his old friend Inspector Gilbert Bodwin. Stanwick was in London for a week to attend a Churchill Society dinner in Pall Mall.

"I expect this must be a particularly busy time for you," Stanwick continued, "with the foreign ministers' conference only a week away."

Bodwin leaned forward intently across his desk. "It is indeed, and that's why I'm glad to have a chance to talk with you."

"Oh?" Stanwick finished lighting his pipe and peered at Bodwin curiously through a cloud of smoke.

"Yes, and the Prime Minister is furious at the breach in security. Some important state papers were taken from a safe at the Foreign and Commonwealth Office two nights ago, at about nine-thirty. From the way it was done, we know the thief had to have known the combination of the safe.

"We have three suspects. They are all clerks in the FCO: James Malcolm, Samuel Hickory, and William Dell. Each knows the combination as part of his duties." Stanwick, full of interest, absentmindedly fingered a tip of his mustache.

"Of course you've questioned them," he said. "Just what accounts do they give of their whereabouts on the evening of the theft?"

Bodwin flipped open a notebook. "Malcolm says he went to the theatre with his wife that evening."

The inspector produced four scraps of paper, which Stanwick recognized as the halves of two torn tickets.

"He showed us these from his jacket pocket," Bodwin went on. "As you can see, they are for that evening's eight o'clock performance of *Coningsby* at the Disraeli Playhouse in Southwark. The play lasted until ten, and the ushers say no one left early. The Malcolms live in Chiswick and say they travelled to and from the theatre in their own car.

"Hickory maintains that he was engrossed in a darts tournament at his neighborhood pub from eight until eleven that night. That's the Sacred Cow in St. John's Wood. I have statements here from several of the regulars, all of whom confirm that Hickory was there the whole time."

"Does he often play darts there?" asked Stanwick.

"The regulars say he stops by about twice a week for an evening pint," Bodwin replied, "but he hardly ever plays darts."

"How about Dell?"

"He's the only one without an alibi that we could readily verify. He lives alone and says he spent the whole evening watching television. He told my sergeant the plots of all that evening's BBC1 programs, but he's still our prime suspect. There just isn't anything solid to go on."

"Does he also live in town?"

Bodwin nodded. "Small flat in Belgrave Road. Any suggestions? The P. M. will want my head on a platter if we don't nab our man."

Stanwick laughed and languidly stood up.

"I'm ready for a bite of lunch," he said. "If you'll join me in a stroll to the little pub I saw down the street, I'll be glad to tell you the identity of the thief."

WHO STOLE THE DOCUMENTS?

Solution on page 252.

THE EXPLORER'S TALE

Thomas P. Stanwick, the amateur logician, had seldom been so surprised or delighted.

In return for what he considered a few tri-fling deductions that had helped avert the disruption of an important state con-ference in London, the Queen had given him free passage back to the United States aboard a luxury passenger liner.

Stanwick quickly fell into the routine on board and began to enjoy the cruise thoroughly. By day he strode the deck, read, played games, or leaned against the railing and gazed out at the dark waters of the North Atlantic. By night he dined in elegance with the other passengers and then relaxed in one of the ship's lounges, engrossed in conversation, chess, cards, or a good book.

On the evening of the sixth day, Stanwick was sitting in a com-fortable armchair and listening to a long travelogue by Gregory Justin, a self-proclaimed adventurer and explorer. Justin, a stout, middle-aged man with a ruddy face and thinning red hair, leaned toward Stanwick and spoke with obvious relish.

"Later that year," he went on, "I led an expedition of 20 on a photographic tour of the jungles and plains of Zambia. We were there almost three months, and what a time we had! The jungles were dark and beautiful but safe enough, as long as we were careful about the occasional snake or tiger that crossed our path. On the plain, though, we once had a pretty harrowing night.

"We had spent that day photographing an elephant herd and a pride of lions. The male lions slept most of the day, but when they shook their great manes and looked up, they were a magnificent sight.

"We made camp that night on the plain, about two miles from the pride. At two-thirty, I was awakened by some yelling. A rogue lioness with a dangerous appetite had found our camp and was clawing at some of the tents. I looked out and could see her in the moonlight, so I grabbed my rifle, got her in my sights, and put her down. I hated to do it, but it was necessary."

"You had quite an exciting time, I guess," remarked Stanwick with a smile. He arose lazily and shook hands with Justin. "Thank you. I enjoyed your stories. I have some letters to write this evening, so I'll now wish you a good night."

Before returning to his cabin, Stanwick stepped out on deck and strolled to the railing. A few sparks from his pipe danced out into the inky void.

"Justin's a fine storyteller," he muttered to himself. "It's a pity his stories aren't entirely true!"

WHAT FLAW DID STANWICK FIND IN JUSTIN'S STORY?

Solution on page 252.

THE CASE OF THE REINDEER SPIES

The ringing of the doorbell cut through the clacking of the keyboard in Thomas P. Stanwick's small study. The amateur logician arose from the history textbook he was editing and went to the door. Rufus, his black labrador, lifted his head sleepily from his paws.

"Mr. Stanwick?" A tall man in a brown suit flashed a badge. "I'm Special Agent Stevens of the F.E.I. Inspector Walker of the Royston Police referred me to you. Do you mind if I come in?"

"Not at all." Though surprised by the visit, Stanwick showed Stevens into the living room with quiet geniality. It was not the first time that he had received unusual visitors through Walker's recommendations.

Stevens glanced curiously around at the crowded bookshelves, the wall maps, and the papers and dusty chess sets piled on various side tables. Declining Stanwick's offer of tea, he seated himself in an armchair near the hearth. Stanwick sat down in an armchair across from him and relit his pipe.

"Matt Walker is a good friend of mine, Mr.

Stevens," he said, "and I'm always glad to help him or an associate of his if I can. I presume that in this case I may be of some service to the government."

"Exactly, Mr. Stanwick," replied Stevens. "I've come to you because this case has a tangled knot of facts, and Walker says you can untangle such knots better than anyone else he knows. We are also aware, of course, of your past services to the American and British governments.

"Briefly, the facts are these. As a result of the national effort to crack down on domestic spies, the Bureau has uncovered a ring of five spies in Royston who have started selling defense industry secrets to the Chinese consulate in New York. The five individuals have been identified, and we are intercepting their messages.

"We believe they may be able to lead us to several similar rings in the Midwest, so we want to continue monitoring their messages a while longer before we arrest them. Our problem is that they refer to each other in code names, and we need to match the individuals to the code names before we can completely understand the messages."

Stanwick reached lazily for a pad of paper and a pencil. "What do you have so far?" he asked.

Stevens opened a notebook.

"The code names," he said with a slight smile, "are those of well-known reindeer: Comet, Cupid, Dasher, Dancer, and Donder. We are certain that these names correspond in some order to the members of the group, all of whom live in Royston.

"Sal Abelardo is a civil engineer for Spacetech. His wife works for a publishing company and apparently knows nothing of his espionage activities. Peter Bircham works as a janitor for the same firm.

He is single. John Cantrell is a junior executive with Aeroco. He and his wife share a condo downtown with his sister. Tim Delmarin, unmarried, is a communications expert with the same firm. The fifth member is Telly Ephesos, a retired Foreign Service Officer who spent twenty years in China. He is married and has no siblings."

Stanwick puffed on his pipe and wrote quietly on the pad, while Rufus delicately sniffed the visitor's briefcase.

"From the messages already sent," continued Stevens, "and our own investigation, we've been able to glean only a few facts. Cantrell and 'Dasher' and their wives sometimes take vacations together. 'Cupid' is highly dissatisfied with his job. Mrs. Abelardo regularly corresponds with 'Mrs. Donder.' Neither 'Comet' nor 'Dasher' has ever been outside the state. Mrs. Abelardo was once engaged to the brother of 'Donder.' Finally, Bircham makes monthly trips to Mexico City.

"I cannot impress upon you enough, Mr. Stanwick, the importance of identifying these code names. Any help you could give us in this matter would be greatly appreciated."

Stanwick, too preoccupied to answer immediately, paused and fingered a tip of his mustache as languid wisps of smoke curled up from his pipe. A moment later he scribbled something on his pad and tossed it to Stevens.

"Here are the code names and their possessors. Happy hunting!"

WHO HAS WHICH CODE NAME?

Solution on page 252.

STANWICK AND THE
ACCIDENTAL THIEF

Thomas P. Stanwick roamed the Christmas-lit aisles of Schweppe's Department Store, looking for the right gift for his old friend Annie Tynsdale. Annie owned a candy shop in Cambridge, England.

The women's accessories aisle seemed safe enough. He strolled down it slowly, eying successive displays of purses, handkerchiefs, wallets, coin purses, scarves, and gloves.

Though the prices on the tags were unexpectedly high, the goods were all handsome and of good quality. He paused by the glove table and picked up a pair.

Just then a small commotion at the front of the store attracted his attention. Jim Sperlich, the store detective, had just re-entered the store grasping a young blond woman firmly by the arm. In his other hand he held a brown leather coin purse. The woman, her face flushed, struggled to free her arm.

"Let me go, you gorilla," she spat. "I was going to pay for it!"

"We'll let the store manager decide," Sperlich replied stolidly. "Just come along, please." He guided her toward a small office in the back of the store.

Stanwick, who knew both Sperlich and the store manager, Dale Carpenter, decided to be on hand. Putting down the gloves, he strode to Carpenter's office, which was closer to him than to Sperlich and his captive.

"Merry Christmas, Dale!" he exclaimed to Carpenter, who looked up from his papers with a start. "How's business these days?"

"Hello, Tom! Why, it's not too—"

"Excuse me, Mr. Carpenter." Sperlich arrived with the woman, and Stanwick smiled and smoothly stepped to a corner of the office. "Hi, Tom. I caught this lady shoplifting, Mr. Carpenter. I spotted her just as she was thrusting this coin purse into her jacket pocket, and stayed near her until she left the premises without paying for it. Then I apprehended her."

"It's all an innocent mistake!" exclaimed the woman, wrenching her arm free at last and facing Carpenter angrily. "I intended to pay for it. I'm just absent-minded, and forgot at the last minute that I had it."

Carpenter took the coin purse and quickly examined its leather exterior. Snapping it open, he checked the lining and extracted the price tag.

"One of our better brands of ladies' coin purses," he noted. "May I ask, Ms.—"

"Leonard. Celia Leonard."

"May I ask, Ms. Leonard, why you put this purse in your pocket?"

"I tucked it away—temporarily—because I wanted to try on a few pairs of gloves, and so needed to free my hands." She turned angrily to Sperlich. "Isn't that right, Mr. Hot Shot Detective? If you were staying so close to me, you must have seen me try on the gloves."

Sperlich's face flushed a little.

"Well, it's true, Mr. Carpenter," he replied. "After putting the purse in her pocket, she did try on three or four pairs of gloves. And put them all back."

"See there?" She smiled at the manager in cold triumph. "Now please let me pay for or return the coin purse and be on my way."

Carpenter scratched his balding head. "Well, I don't know. Technically, of course, you are guilty of shoplifting by leaving the store without paying for the item, whether or not you intended to do so. However, since there seems to be good reason to believe that it wasn't intentional, maybe —"

"Just a moment, Dale." Stanwick interrupted him and stepped forward. "This lady's theft of the coin purse was quite intentional, and I think you should press charges."

HOW DOES STANWICK KNOW THAT
SHE INTENDED TO STEAL THE PURSE?

Solution on page 252.

THE McPHERSON-McTAVISH MYSTERY

Early one drizzly morning, as Thomas P. Stanwick was finishing breakfast at the White Lion Inn, the innkeeper told him he was wanted on the phone. This surprised him, since he was on the third day of a vacation in Dartmoor, England, and few people knew he was there.

"Mr. Stanwick? This is Inspector Carstairs," said the voice on the phone.

"Oh, yes." The amateur logician had met the inspector at the local pub two days earlier and had swapped crime stories with him. "What can I do for you?"

"Colonel Rogers was murdered in his library last evening. Since you've been helpful in other police investigations, I thought you might be interested in dropping by and having a look at this one."

"Thank you, Carstairs. I'd be delighted."

The Rogers estate was only two miles across the moor from the inn, so within an hour Stanwick had walked to the main house, scraped the sticky red clay of the moor from his feet, and joined Carstairs in the library. Colonel Rogers lay in front of his desk, shot in the chest at point-blank range.

Carstairs pointed to two grizzled, middle-aged men sitting sullenly nearby.

"That's McTavish on the right and McPherson on the left. McTavish is a neighbor and McPherson is the groundskeeper here. McTavish says he saw McPherson bury the murder weapon, a shotgun, in the garden last evening."

"That's right, sir," cried McTavish. "I had my telescope set up just a few miles away on a little knoll on the moor. Before lookin' out at the stars, I swung it around the landscape a bit—to test it, you know. That's when I saw him come out, look around, and bury the gun."

"A rotten lie!" roared McPherson. "I was in my cottage all evening until the constable came knocking last night."

"That's enough!" Carstairs warned. "We dug up that shotgun last night from the spot in the garden that McTavish showed us. All indications are that it's the murder weapon."

Stanwick examined the dirty shotgun leaning against the wall. Beside the shotgun was a golf bag with a broken strap, scuffed along the bottom but otherwise unmarked. Inside, however, Stanwick found no clubs, but telescopic equipment instead.

"Is this your golf bag, Mr. McTavish?" he asked.

"Aye. Every week for months now, I've dragged that bag with my telescope from the village up to the knoll to look at the stars."

"Wasn't it too cloudy last night for that?"

"No, it rained a bit in the afternoon, but by dusk it had cleared some."

"How could you see Mr. McPherson at night?"

"Oh, at dusk it was still light enough to see what he was doin'."

Stanwick sat down in a nearby armchair and fingered the tip of his mustache.

"Mr. McPherson," he asked, "did you hear a shot last night?"

"No, sir," was the reply. "My cottage is some distance from the library."

"Who called you, Carstairs?"

"I received a call from McTavish, who said he had just rushed back to the village. We picked him up with his equipment, came here, discovered the body, and found the gun where he said McPherson had buried it."

"Any fingerprints?"

"None left on the gun, and only those of the colonel in the room. Also, the housekeeper tells me an ivory-handled knife is missing from his desk."

"Well, well." Stanwick abruptly arose and faced McTavish. "I think you had better start telling the truth, Mr. McTavish. Your story is a lie!"

HOW DOES STANWICK KNOW
MCTAVISH IS LYING?

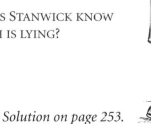

Solution on page 253.

MURDER IN
A LONDON FLAT

Lord Calinore was gunned down in his London flat by a robber, who then ransacked the flat. The case was placed in the capable hands of Inspector Gilbert Bodwin of Scotland Yard. Bodwin's investigation revealed that one man had planned the

crime, another had carried it out, and a third had acted as lookout.

Bodwin discussed the case at length one evening over dinner at his club with an old friend, Thomas P. Stanwick, the amateur logician, visiting from America.

"It's quite a case," Stanwick remarked. "Have you any suspects?"

Bodwin sliced his roast beef with rel-ish. "Yes, indeed. Four. We have conclusive evidence that three of those four were responsible for the crime."

"Really! That's remarkable progress. What about the fourth?"

"He had no prior knowledge of the crime and is completely innocent. The problem is that we're not sure which of the four are the planner, the gunman, the lookout, and the innocent bystander."

"I see." Stanwick took more Yorkshire pudding. "What do you know about them at this point?"

"Well, the names of the four are Merrick, Cross, Llewellyn, and Halifax. Halifax and Cross play golf together every Saturday. They're an odd pair! Halifax can't drive, and Cross has been out of Dartmoor Prison for only a year."

"What was he in for?"

"Forgery. We know that Merrick and Halifax kept the flat under surveillance for several days just before the day the crime was committed, the 17th. Llewellyn and Merrick, with their wives, had dinner together on the Strand on the 12th."

"An interesting compilation," said Stanwick, "but hardly conclusive. Is that all of it?"

"Not quite. We know that the gunman spent the week before the crime in Edinburgh, and that the innocent bystander was acquainted with the planner and the gunman, but not with the lookout."

"That is very helpful," said Stanwick with a smile. He raised his wine glass. "Bodwin, old fellow, your case is complete."

WHO ARE THE PLANNER, THE GUNMAN, AND THE LOOKOUT?

Solution on page 253.

THE MATTER OF THE MCALISTER MURDERS

Whit Knowlton, a retired lawyer in his eighties, loved to reminisce about his trials. His memory was shaky, however, and he sometimes had to let his listeners fill in blank spots in his narrative.

One lazy Sunday afternoon in the summer, Knowlton was sitting in his well-stocked library swapping stories with Thomas P. Stanwick. The amateur logician always enjoyed his visits with Knowlton.

"The McAlister murders in Baltimore hit the papers in the winter of 1953," said the lawyer. "Four men were arrested for the murders within a week, and I was called in to assist the district attorney.

"All four were indicted, but evidence brought out in the

course of the trial proved that only two of them were guilty. Our problem was to find out which two they were."

"How useful was their testimony?" asked Stanwick.

"Oh, useful enough, as it turned out," Knowlton replied. "The first defendant, Addler, said that either the second defendant, Byran, was guilty, or the fourth defendant, Derrick, was innocent. Byran said that he was innocent, and that either Addler or Collins, the third defendant, was guilty.

"Collins said that Byran and Derrick were not both guilty. Derrick, after a long refusal to speak at all, said that Collins was innocent if and only if Addler was also innocent."

"Were any of their statements proven true?" Stanwick asked.

"Well, yes. Other evidence proved that the two guilty ones were lying and the two innocent ones were telling the truth. Unfortunately, I don't quite remember anymore who the guilty ones were."

Stanwick smiled and fumbled in his pocket for his pipe.

"This case is a treat, Whit," he said, "for it's not too hard to deduce who the guilty ones were."

WHO WERE THE GUILTY ONES?

Solution on page 253.

DEATH IN THE GARAGE

Inspector Matthew Walker and Thomas P. Stanwick had barely begun their weekly game that Thursday evening at the chess club when Walker's beeper went off.

"There's been a suspicious death in Caterina Road," said Walker when he returned from the phone. "Probably a suicide. Care to come?"

"By all means. Some evenings weren't made for chess."

A quarter of an hour later, Walker and Stanwick were in the garage of Walter McCarthy, a real estate broker. McCarthy was seated behind the wheel of his car, dead. The garage door was open, the car was silent, and the police were busily at work.

"The body was discovered by Mrs. McCarthy when she returned home on foot about six," reported Sergeant Hatch. "The car was running. Nearly overcome by exhaust fumes herself, she opened the garage door from the inside, switched off the car, and

called 9-1-1 from the kitchen. She's inside now."

"Cause of death established?" asked Walker.

"The medical examiner says the body shows every sign of carbon monoxide asphyxiation. We did find these in the right jacket pocket, though." Hatch handed Walker a plastic evidence bag containing a pill bottle. Walker gingerly removed the bottle, glanced at the label, and popped open the cap. The bottle was half full of large, pink lozenges.

"A prescription depressant," he remarked. "Refilled only yesterday for one pill a day, and yet half the pills are gone. Could these have killed him?"

"No, they couldn't," responded Dr. Pillsbury, the owlish medical examiner, who now approached Walker. "If he took half the bottle, though, the dose would have knocked him out in about fifteen seconds."

"But why would he take the pills if he were about to asphyxiate himself anyway?" asked Stanwick. "Asphyxiation is painless."

Pillsbury shrugged. "It is. But he may have wanted to put himself under sooner, before he could lose his nerve. I've seen it before in suicides."

"Hatch," said Walker, turning to the sergeant, "what was found in the car?"

"Nothing unusual, sir. Registration, maps, ice scraper, a scarf, a bag of chips. A folder of house listings. In the trunk, some tools, a spare, jumper cables, a blanket."

"Has a suicide note turned up?"

"Not yet, sir. We're still checking the house."

"And how much gas was in the tank?" asked Stanwick.

"Oh, plenty, sir. More than enough."

"Thank you, sergeant," said Walker. "Please tell Mrs. McCarthy I'll see her soon."

"Yes, sir."

As Hatch strode off, Walker turned back to Stanwick.

"Well, Tom, I'm afraid there's not much of special interest here. Whether or not we find a note, this looks to me like a straightforward suicide."

Stanwick shook his head solemnly.

"I don't think so, Matt," he replied. "Though I can't be certain, I think this is a case of murder."

Why does Stanwick think McCarthy was murdered?

Solution on page 254.

MURDER AT THE CHESSBOARD

Thomas P. Stanwick and Inspector Matthew Walker were seated one afternoon in Stanwick's living room, chatting about recent crime news.

"You may have seen something in the papers," said Walker, "about the murder two nights ago of Professor Richard Hansford."

"Yes, I think so." Stanwick frowned. "The archaeologist. He was stabbed in the back while seated at a chessboard in his study, wasn't he? Killed instantly."

"That's right. A call came in to headquarters at 8:30 last Wednesday night from Michael Rimbach, a visiting relative of Hansford's.

"When the squad car arrived, Rimbach explained to the officers that he had heard a cry from the study as he was passing by in the hallway. Looking in, he saw the professor slumped back in his chair and caught a glimpse of a man escaping through the French doors of the study onto the lawn. Rimbach rushed to the doors, but the man had already disappeared into the rainy darkness.

"Hansford was obviously dead, so without touching anything, Rimbach called the police and told Hansford's sister Emily of the crime. Emily, an invalid, had heard nothing.

"Rimbach thinks he recognized the man as David Kunst, a neighbor who played chess with Hansford every Wednesday evening at 7:30. They were both enthusiasts of monochromatic chess, and played no other kind."

"Really?" said Stanwick. "Chess in which no piece can move from a black square to a white square, or vice versa? That's quite rare."

"Yes, it is, which is why they played it so regularly. It's hard to find partners for it. Rimbach, the sister, and Kunst all confirmed the weekly games.

"When we interviewed Kunst at his home later that evening," Walker continued, "he said he had received a call from Rimbach a little after seven saying that Hansford was ill and had to cancel that evening's game. Kunst said he therefore spent the evening at home. Rimbach denies having called him. Kunst lives alone, and there were no witnesses. We saw a damp overcoat and shoes there, but he says they got wet on his way home from work."

"In what condition did you find the study?" Stanwick asked.

"The French doors were open. We looked for footprint traces

on the lawn, but found nothing definite. The condition of the board indicated that a game was in progress when the murder occurred."

"Did the board look like the game had been in progress for an hour?"

"Yes, I guess so. It looked like the players were entering the middle part of the game. A knight and two bishops were already posted in the center of the board."

"Had the weekly game ever been called off before?"

"Now and then. Usually the sister phoned Kunst if Hansford was ill. She had been confined to her bed that day, though, and hadn't seen her brother."

"Well," said Stanwick, fingering the tip of his mustache, "you have an interesting but thoroughly contradictory pair of stories to consider. One of them is patently untrue, however, so I suggest you concentrate your inquiry in the direction of the liar."

WHO IS LYING?

Solution on page 254.

MATCH WITS
WITH
INSPECTOR FORSOOTH

MEET YOUR COLLEAGUE

Are you ready for something a bit more challenging? Something new and different? You've come to the right place. Grab your hat (I'm never without my own wide-brimmed number, like the ones Bogart used to wear) and work with me on these mysteries that are like no others you've tried.
Read the mystery text and then fire questions at yours truly—Inspector Forsooth, Sleuth Extraordinaire. By the way, I do my best thinking when I'm working with a yo-yo . . . you might want to give that a try, yourself!

Sound interesting? Good. It gets even better.

These mysteries go far beyond the "one-shot wonder" format. Such mysteries can be entertaining—I've worked on hundreds of them myself. But each one of the mysteries here contains a mosaic of clues that the sleuth (that's YOU, now!) must piece together to divine the solution. I'll give you a hand in the question-and-answer session that flushes out each and every tiny clue hidden in the text. You can read all the answers or test yourself by reading only a few. It's all up to you.

I feel I should warn you, though. These mysteries are hard! They're not child's play. But I'm confident you'll love the challenges I have in store for you.

MURDER AROUND THE CLOCK

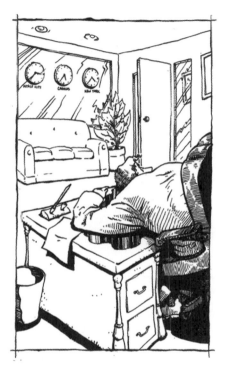

Bruce Berringer was a successful man, but he paid a high price. When all was said and done, his success cost him his life.

Berringer was born and raised in the small town of Bogusville, near the Colorado/Utah border. His was a blue-collar community, and the townsfolk were the sort of friendly, hardworking, generous souls that so often come out of rural America. But Berringer wanted more. He wanted money, prestige, and a name for himself in international business circles.

He had the smarts, the drive, and the connections to make good on his dream. His father was a Navy man who had traveled all over the world prior to returning to Bogusville, and Bruce's business savvy parlayed these far-flung contacts into a thriving importing enterprise: pottery, belts, wicker—you name it. Berringer Imports grew to the point where it had satellite offices literally around the world. But rather than leave his roots,

Berringer delighted in keeping his main office right at home, knowing he could parade his success in front of all those who thought he'd never amount to anything in this world.

CARACAS

As a result of Berringer's obsession with fame, friendships suffered. His childhood cronies noticed that Berringer judged them by what they did for a living and not who they were as people. None of them made one-tenth the money Berringer did, and his scorn was always there.

One night there was a big party at Berringer Imports to celebrate the landing of a new international account. Five of Bruce's friends from high school showed up. They didn't necessarily want to be there, and they certainly didn't fit in with the corporate types who flew in for the occasion; but in some sense it was worse to be left out of the lavish Berringer celebrations than to suffer through one night. Liked or not, Berringer was the most powerful figure in town, and he could be very vengeful when people didn't play the games he wanted them to.

The cronies included Rafael Betz, who owned a catering business and was doing well in his own right, in no small part because he had the opportunity to cater many of Berringer's parties, including this particular one. Then there was Frank Dowling, a plumbing contractor, who complained that the ultra-rich Berringer was incredibly cheap, haggling over charges that normal people would pay without comment. The other local guests were rated even lower on Berringer's importance scale. There was Sean McGillicuddy, whose DairyFresh route took him to the outskirts of the Berringer estate but never any farther, and there was Jimmie Wu, who scratched out a living by refereeing local high school athletic contests, including many involving Berringer's spoiled son Yancey. About the only one of Berringer's buddies who looked comfortable at this black-tie affair was Benjamin Walters, but only because he was accustomed to formalities. Walters was the maître d' at the swank Olivia's restaurant, which was starting with money from—you guessed it—Bruce Berringer. Berringer even got a rare laugh by raising his arm and calling out "Maître d'!" upon spying Walters at the party in his usual tuxedo.

Most of the guests had a decent enough time that night. The oyster bar was fully stocked, and the champagne was flowing. But trouble lurked. After the party, Berringer went back to his desk at the other side of the office complex to tidy up some unfinished business, never mind how late it was. He was discovered the next morn-

NEW YORK

ing, sitting at his desk, with two gunshot wounds in his chest. He was as dead as a doornail. The time of his death was later estimated to be between midnight and 2:00 a.m., Mountain Time.

The most curious aspect of the crime scene was a note that Berringer had left on the pink notepad on his desk. The note said simply: "1:30 hence . . . ," then it trailed off. The note had presumably been written after the shots were fired, in the limited amount of time that he had remaining.

Because Berringer's five school buddies were the last people to leave the party, they were considered the primary suspects. It turned out that four of them had gone out after the party, and each could vouch for the others' whereabouts. When told about Berringer's note, they confirmed that they were still together at 1:30. The only exception was Jimmie Wu, who didn't like the idea of all-night carousing, given that he was supposed to be a stern, proper official for the community. Wu insisted that he had gone straight to bed, but he had no one who could corroborate his story.

When Inspector Forsooth visited the crime scene, he looked up at the wall outside Berringer's office. There, through the glass, he saw a row of clocks, each displaying the time at one of Berringer Imports' offices around the world. First there was a clock labeled "Chicago," which was Berringer's first office outside of Bogusville. The row continued with the other six office sites, in order of their establishment: Paris, Los Angeles, Cairo, Mexico City, Caracas, and New York. Berringer liked to be able to look up from his office and see immediately what the time was throughout his empire. That way he could keep even better tabs on all his regional managers, all of whom he lorded over like a drill sergeant.

Forsooth studied the clocks as if in a trance, until one of the other detectives interrupted him. "Inspector, you okay?" Forsooth nodded. The detective then asked, "Any idea how we're going to locate the killer?" There was a short pause, and then Forsooth issued a curiously short reply:

"Time will tell."

1) Who killed Bruce Berringer?

2) How can the other suspects be ruled out?

INSPECTOR FORSOOTH ANSWERS YOUR QUESTIONS

Q1—Were the clocks digital or analog?

They were analog. Had the clocks been digital, the killer might still be loose! (Remember, all the questions are actual questions from online sleuths. They didn't have the benefit of the illustration at the beginning of this story!)

Q2—If the high school cronies hated Berringer, why were they at the party?

Because Berringer was a vindictive, petty man, and there was no telling what he might do if they didn't show up to admire his wealth. Better to grin and bear it through one night.

Q3—Did it matter that Berringer's father was in the Navy?

Yes. It meant that Berringer was familiar with the concept of a distress signal, which is precisely what he was trying to convey in his note.

Q4—Was the murder committed at 1:30?

No, it was not.

Q5—Is the order of the clocks important?

Absolutely. Theoretically, though, you could deduce the answer without knowing the order!

Q6—Is the number of clocks important?

Even more important than the order, in some sense. The fact that there were seven clocks is central to the solution.

Q7—Were the clocks arranged in some sort of code?

They sure were. Semaphore code, to be precise, which Berringer probably picked up from his father.

Q8—Do you need to know semaphore code to be able to solve the mystery?

No, you do not—would I do that to you? All you need to know is that semaphore code is given using flags and different positions of the arms—much like the hands of a clock. Each letter of the alphabet can be depicted by a specific position of the flags—or hands, as the case may be.

Q9—Dowling and Walters are the only two suspects whose names have seven letters. Does this mean one of them killed Bruce Berringer?

Believe it or not, the length of their names is not important.

Q10—Is the location of the offices important?

In general, no. But the location of a couple of them can lead you to the murderer.

Q11—When did the murder actually take place?

The murder took place at just after midnight. The "hence" in Berringer's note meant "in the future," not "therefore." You could use semaphore code to determine the precise time!

Q12—Is it significant that Berringer addressed Walters as "Maître d'"?

Yes, it's extremely significant. Remember, Berringer cared more about what people did than who they were. But in order to identify the killer, you're still going to have to supply one teensy-weensy ingredient that hasn't been covered in these 12 questions.

CAN YOU SOLVE THE MYSTERY?

Solution on page 255.

TIMING IS EVERYTHING

The case started out as a robbery but ended up as a homicide. On the face of it, that's not the strangest combination in the world. But in this case the person who was robbed wasn't the person who was murdered!

Early one Saturday morning, in the country town of Cedarville, a man named Buford Huxley reported that his toolshed had been broken into. The shed was secured by an ordinary combination lock that had been cleanly severed, probably with a pair of bolt cutters. The shed was located right outside Huxley's barn, and was where he kept all sorts of gardening tools—rakes, hoes, and the like. But most important of all was that he kept a set of hunting rifles there, and one of them was missing. That item was of particular interest to Inspector Forsooth upon his arrival that morning.

Forsooth knew something that Huxley might not have known.

What Forsooth knew was that a man named James Hooligan, who lived about 30 minutes away, had been murdered just the night before by a rifle shot that came through the window of his home. And that set the stage for an interesting exchange.

Shortly after Forsooth arrived at Huxley's place, Muriel Huxley came out to the barn screaming, "Did you hear what happened?!" She had been listening to an all-news radio station while doing some gardening, and had heard the account of the murder. When she saw Forsooth, she backed off a bit, and he assumed it was because her hands and face were quite dirty; she apologized for her appearance, explaining that she had just finished planting some 300 daffodil bulbs along a stone wall behind their house. However, Forsooth wasn't too concerned with how she looked, because there was more to this story than met the eye.

Buford Huxley seemed strangely self-conscious upon hearing of Hooligan's death. It was clear that Hooligan was no stranger to this household, and the ties grew deeper as the investigation progressed. For one, the murder weapon was discovered in a wooded area about halfway between the Huxley and Hooligan residences. It was Huxley's missing rifle, all right, and ballistics tests confirmed that it was the source of the fatal shots. Separately, police uncovered a pair of slightly rusty bolt cutters not far from the rifle. Huxley admitted that the gun was his, but denied any part in the shooting. However, the Huxleys had to own up to some crucial and somewhat embarrassing facts upon further questioning.

According to Muriel Huxley, James Hooligan had been blackmailing her husband and two other men, Edgar Plotz and Dinky Martinez, for their participation in a kickback scheme several years before, when her husband worked for Acme Construction Company: Plotz and Martinez had given Huxley kickbacks in return for Huxley's selecting their then-struggling roofing company as a major subcontractor on projects spearheaded by Acme. Buford Huxley now worked with Plotz and Martinez in their own concrete-pouring venture, and part of the Huxley barn had been converted into an office for that venture. Hooligan had managed to figure out that the seed money for his new enterprise had come illegally.

Huxley at first denied the plot, but he conceded that he had received a threatening letter from Hooligan just days before. He also said that it was only a coincidence that the shed had been locked in the first place. He said he had gotten into an argument with his wife and obtained a lock so that she couldn't access her precious gardening tools—the rifles were the last things on his mind! He acknowledged that his two business partners were the only other people who even knew about the lock, but he was quick to add that he alone knew the combination.

The night of Hooligan's death, Huxley had held a meeting with his "coconspirators," Plotz and Martinez. The subject, of course:

what to do about the blackmailing. Plotz had arrived at 8:45, Martinez at 9:00. The meeting lasted for about an hour, with no specific plan but a lot of anger and fear all around. Huxley admitted that his two friends had talked about giving Hooligan some "concrete boots," but he didn't take their bluster very seriously. Huxley also said that he had gone back to his house after the meeting. He assumed that the others had left immediately and hadn't come back, but he admitted that he wasn't sure. However, he could confirm that the lock was quite intact when he left the meeting.

The coroner determined that James Hooligan had died sometime the prior night, but it wasn't possible to pinpoint the time of death any more than that. One potentially helpful detail came from one of Hooligan's neighbors, who had been walking her dog about 10:30. She reported that a light was on in Hooligan's downstairs bathroom, but as she walked by, that light went off. Interestingly, Hooligan's body was found in the downstairs den, whose window was right next to the bathroom window. The shot that killed Hooligan had been fired from the outside, as evidenced by a shattered windowpane and some glass fragments found in the den. When investigators arrived the next morning, the den light was still on, and the bathroom light was still off.

Dinky Martinez—who, despite his name, was a strong, stocky fellow—said he returned to his home at just before midnight, a time his wife confirmed. When asked what he did after the meeting broke up, he said that he had gone out to a neighborhood bar to shoot, er, play some pool. In fact, he had told his wife he'd been playing pool all night, to conceal the true nature of his business.

Edgar Plotz, the ringleader of the embezzlement scheme,

claimed he had gone directly home after the meeting, arriving there at about 10:30. Because he lived alone, there was no one who could corroborate his story. He added that he didn't know a rifle from a bulb planter, but his lawyer cut him off before he could say more; now that the kickbacks were common knowledge, Plotz needed all the counsel he could get.

As for Huxley, he admitted that his wife was asleep when he got in after the meeting, so she couldn't vouch for him, but he insisted he didn't go anywhere.

Well, are you ready? Here are your questions:

1) Who killed James Hooligan?

2) Explain the key elements of timing in this case.

3) What was the missing piece of evidence that tied the murderer to the crime?

INSPECTOR FORSOOTH ANSWERS YOUR QUESTIONS

Q1—If the murder occurred after 10:30, would that implicate Dinky Martinez?

Yes, it sure would. Everyone else seems to have alibis for that time period, with the possible exception of Buford Huxley.

Q2—What time of year did the murder take place?

Presumably it was in the late fall, because Muriel Huxley was struggling to get all her daffodil bulbs planted before the ground froze. But the precise time of year isn't important.

Q3—Was the light hit by a shot from the rifle?
No, it wasn't. The only shots went through the window of the adjacent den. But knowing why the light went out would be very helpful regarding the timing of this case. Remember the title!

Q4—Was the murder related to the embezzlement?
Only indirectly. Sorry to be vague, but that's a clue in and of itself.

Q5—Would it have been possible for Buford Huxley to have gone to Hooligan's house without his wife's knowing?
Absolutely. She was sound asleep.

Q6—Could Muriel have cut the lock after the meeting ended?
No, for the same reason as the answer to #5 above.

Q7—Could Buford Huxley have cut the lock himself, to make it look as though someone were framing him?
It is entirely possible, although there is no evidence to back that up. Wouldn't that be clever?

Q8—Was the lock the same one bought by Huxley?
Yes, it was. Great question, though.

Q9—Was the murder actually announced on the radio?
It sure was. Muriel was entirely legit.

Q10—Had Plotz ever been inside the toolshed?
It sure looks that way, judging by his comment about the rifle and the bulb planter. As for when he might have been inside, well,

that's something that your supersleuth abilities should figure out.

Q11—Was the neighbor sure about the time the light went out?
Positive.

Q12—Why were the bolt cutters rusty?
Because they had been outside longer than you might have thought.

CAN YOU SOLVE THE MYSTERY?

Solution on page 257.

THE PIANO REQUITAL

As Gilbert von Stade performed, there wasn't an aficionado in the house who didn't marvel at his mastery of the keyboard. Von Stade was playing Chopin's Etude in G flat, Opus 10, no. 5, a most challenging piece by anyone's standards, even for a world-class pianist such as von Stade. The piece wasn't particularly long, as a number of performers were being showcased that night in a concert to benefit the city's sagging Foundation for the Arts. Yet it was a spell-binding few minutes.

When his work was done, von Stade got up from the piano to acknowledge a raucous standing ovation, which had become the norm at his performances. He was loved by virtually all who followed the music world; whereas other musicians of his talent tended to be aloof, he was known for being gracious and generous with his time. He took delight in the crowd, and always mingled after his concerts. But there was to be no mingling on this particular night. Against the backdrop of the applause, von

Stade suddenly froze up and fell to the stage. The curtain was closed and the show came to a temporary halt. Gilbert von Stade would never regain consciousness.

At first, no one suspected foul play. Gilbert von Stade was a fairly old man, after all, and most everyone in the audience assumed that he had suffered a heart attack. Yet the autopsy would later reveal that his death was anything but natural. Traces of rare but deadly batrachotoxin were found in his system, and had surely been responsible for his death. It was murder, all right, but it remained to determine just who could have committed such a dastardly deed.

It turned out (surprise, surprise) that there was more to the decedent's true character than was ever seen by his adoring public. As is all too often the case within the highest echelon of musical talent, von Stade was an extremely demanding person to work with, and his own search for perfection often victimized those around him. Many thought him hypocritical for basking in the public glory of his music in the wake of exhausting practice sessions in which he had bullied and badgered everyone in sight.

Perhaps because of von Stade's preeminence, there was considerable friction within the group of musicians performing that night. Two younger pianists, Heinrich Albertson and Vivien Frechette, were also on the evening program, and were extremely eager to prove themselves. Albertson had come on before von Stade, and had given an absolutely flawless rendition of another Chopin etude: C major, Opus 10, no. 1. Frechette, on the other hand, was scheduled to play immediately following von Stade, but her performance was delayed by the onstage tragedy. In fact, some of those backstage had qualms about continuing the concert under the circumstances. Stage manager Sophia Brightwell, a frequent target of von Stade's tirades, tried to convince Frechette that it would be inappropriate for her to play, but Frechette would have none of it. She reminded them all that von Stade had been a professional, and had always lived up to the standard that the show must go on.

No one doubted that with von Stade out of the way, Albertson and Frechette had a better chance of success in their own musical careers. However, they certainly weren't the only suspects in the murder, for the rivalry had extended to the people in all of their lives, even if these very people had made a special effort that evening to heal all past wounds.

Marla Albertson, Beatrice von Stade, and Samuel Frechette never completely took to their positions as musicians' spouses. They were still very much in love with their respective mates, but they weren't necessarily attuned to their every note, so to speak. Marla Albertson was especially out of the loop, being unable to read sheet music, much less play it, but she had many other talents. One was cooking, and that night she had organized a pre-concert dinner, full of special culinary treats. She prepared frog's-leg appetizers, and encouraged others to make their own contributions. Samuel Frechette brought some homemade bread and Beatrice von Stade whipped up some linguine with pesto sauce. These offerings were joined by those from many other performers and their families, as the invitees included several dozen musicians who would play that night, not just pianists.

Although everyone applauded Marla for her initiative, the food selections weren't of universal appeal. Some of the musicians had no appetite because of pre-concert nerves, while others were reluctant to get too adventurous with their food choices while dressed in white tie. Among the pianists, only Gilbert von Stade was willing to handle greasy foods such as the frog's legs, but he made a special point of thoroughly washing his hands in the backstage men's room. On the subject of von Stade's food choices, a curious recollection of the evening's emcee, Walter Penwinkle, was that von Stade had garlic on his breath when he collapsed—on his dying breath, at that. Penwinkle and Sophia Brightwell had been the first people to rush to the stricken artist's aid, albeit in a futile cause.

After von Stade's death, the concert was delayed, but it resumed just minutes later with Vivien Frechette at the keyboard, playing Chopin's Etude in E flat minor, Opus 10, no. 6. The piece was slow and melancholy, if not downright mournful, a perfect choice under the circumstances. Then, in a tribute to von Stade, Frechette astonished all the spectators by playing the precise piece von Stade had played earlier. She, too, got a rousing ovation.

Some days later, Inspector Forsooth was called in to unravel the mystery of just what had happened during that ill-fated concert. He paid a visit to the stage where von Stade had fallen, and took time to survey the men's room in the back, where von Stade had washed his hands. There he found soap, toothpaste, mouthwash, some Breath-

Assure tablets, and even a vial of DMSO, which Sophia Brightwell said von Stade used to take for his arthritis, before tiring of its side effects. Forsooth realized that the telling proof behind the von Stade killing might be hard to come by, but now he knew where to look.

1) Who killed Gilbert von Stade?
2) What was the method, and why did it work?
Please be specific!

INSPECTOR FORSOOTH ANSWERS YOUR QUESTIONS

Q1—What is batrachotoxin?

Batrachotoxin is best known as the poison used by some South American tribes to coat their hunting arrows. The poison comes from the secretions of a certain species of tree frog. The natives dipped their arrows into the frog secretions, so even if the arrows didn't cause fatal wounds, the batrachotoxin would. (Not my style, but that's life in the jungle for you.)

Q2—Did Samuel Frechette bring garlic bread to dinner?

Nice try, but no. He brought plain bread.

Q3—How could a food poison get specifically to von Stade if the nonmusicians were eating some of everything?

Good question. I haven't the foggiest idea how that would be possible.

Q4—Does the linguine have garlic in it?

The linguine doesn't have any garlic in it, but the pesto sauce is loaded with it. However, there is a pretty good clue that this didn't kill von Stade.

Q5—Are the pieces played by the pianists relevant?

Yes, they are all relevant.

Q6—What were the unwanted side effects of DMSO?

Nice question. The answer is that von Stade detested the fact that DMSO left him with a garlicky taste in his mouth! (Yes, that's an actual side effect, and it was especially intolerable for von Stade, who liked to mingle with his adoring fans.)

Q7—Does Frechette play with gloves?

No, none of them played with gloves. Another nice question, though!

Q8—Could the pianist who played before him have put the poison onto the keys?

No, that would have been extremely difficult to do, because he was in plain view of the audience the whole time. We have to assume the poison was placed there just before the show began.

Q9—What was so difficult about von Stade's piece?

Ah, I was hoping you would ask. The answer is that the piece is more difficult because it's harder for the fingers to move around on the black keys, which are smaller!

Q10—Did everyone know that piece of music von Stade was

playing that night?
Certainly all the musicians did, and everyone involved with the show did.

Q11—Could the toxin have been absorbed by the skin?
Sure could, if mixed with DMSO. One of the properties of DMSO is that it is readily absorbed through the skin, and in its liquid form is capable of carrying other compounds right along with it.

Q12—Is it possible that the victim was killed by accident, and that one of the other musicians was the actual target?
It's quite possible, and it's a great question. However, that wasn't the case, and it's our job to show how we know that.

CAN YOU SOLVE THE MYSTERY?

Solution on page 258.

THE VALENTINE'S DAY MASSACRE

It was only after Rudy Marcus was killed that his community got a full taste of what his life was really like. Marcus seemed like your average, everyday, strait-laced, white-collar type. A CPA by training, he worked at the Ernst Brothers accounting firm, and by all indications had done quite well for himself.

He had the usual trappings—a nice car and a well-groomed house in the suburbs —all in keeping with his solid-citizen image. But there wasn't much flair to Rudy. Businesswise, Rudy's clients didn't hire him because of his imagination; they hired him for the decimal-point precision with which he approached life. At home, there hadn't been a Mrs. Marcus on the scene for several years. Most people figured she had simply gotten bored.

However, within days of the discovery of Rudy's body, the entire picture changed. One of his neighbors, a Mrs. Cecily Wheelock, revealed that Rudy Marcus was in fact a closet Romeo, a prim accountant by day but a freewheeling bon vivant by night. He was having dalliances with no fewer than three women at the time of his death, each one claiming to be Rudy's real girlfriend. Those three became the focus of an extensive murder investigation.

Fittingly, Rudy had been killed on Valentine's Day, and the murder scene was consistent with a classic crime of passion. Rudy's body lay on the kitchen floor with a knife in his back. The murder weapon was one of his own kitchen knives, which had been taken from its usual resting place on the magnetic rack. It appeared that someone had stabbed Rudy the Romeo when his back was turned. From the absence of a struggle, it was assumed that Rudy knew whomever had murdered him.

The first of Rudy's mistresses to emerge was Cornelia Devane, who worked at the Estée Lauder counter at the nearby Bloomingdale's. Ms. Devane said she had been seeing Rudy for over a year, and was shocked to find out that there could have been other women in his life. But as she reflected on their relationship, she realized that his availability was spo-radic. She had always chalked his busy schedule up to work-related mat-ters, but now she knew better.

Then there was Daphne Nagelson, who had met Rudy the old-fashioned way—as a tax client. She said she was absolutely convinced that Rudy had loved her the most, and to prove it she brought out an emerald brooch he had given her for Valentine's Day. Rudy had bought the brooch while in South America a few months before.

The third of Rudy's girlfriends was Mary Stahl, the only one of the three who was married. She also happened to be a city councilwoman, a highly visible role. Yet no one around her knew of her relationship with Rudy. One interesting aspect of the case, which Stahl shed light on, was that Rudy had been in California on a business trip for several days prior to his murder. Originally, he was supposed to have returned on the 12th, but his client needed more help than he had planned, so he didn't return until the 13th—just one day before he was killed.

Some of the investigators wrinkled their eyebrows upon hearing that little nugget. Apparently they figured that their dead little Casanova might have had something going in other ports as well, but that was never substantiated. Mary Stahl confirmed that Rudy had been thinking about her during his trip, as she brought out a gold necklace he had bought for her while he was away.

It turned out that Rudy had prevailed upon Cornelia Devane to visit his house periodically while he was gone. Her main task was to water the plants, but he also wanted her to turn some lights on and off to thwart any potential burglars, and even to watch TV to give the house a "lived-in" look. Devane said she had done that same routine many times in the past, and expressed some feeling that she had been taken for granted. Rudy hadn't called her while he was gone.

However, he had unexpectedly stopped by her workplace on Valentine's Day to give her a present—a red silk scarf.

Daphne Nagelson told the police that she and Rudy had gone out to see the movie *Bed of Roses* the night before his death, and she produced the ticket stubs to prove it. Cecily Wheelock, the snoopy neighbor, said that Daphne had stopped by Rudy's house earlier on the 13th, and she didn't deny it. But she did deny having gone inside, saying that she'd just stopped by to drop off her Valentine present for Rudy. Mrs. Wheelock confirmed that Daphne had had a little smile on her face when she left the house.

According to the "rotation" that seemed to be developing, that left Mary Stahl as Rudy's companion on the fateful night of February 14th, and, sure enough, she admitted that they, too, had gone to see a movie. When pressed as to the title, she stammered *Dead Man Walking*, not liking the irony of the title one bit. The movie was her treat, so she also had ticket stubs to present, which indicated to the authorities that Rudy was still alive until at least 9:30 p.m., when the movie ended. The coroner had already estimated the time of death as being between 8:00 p.m. and 11:00 p.m., based on the preliminary examination of such factors as rigor mortis and eye fluids. So Rudy clearly didn't live very long after the movie. Stahl also admitted that she'd left a message on Rudy's answering machine the night before he came home. The police located that very message on the machine.

Just when it appeared that the investigation was at a standstill, Inspector Forsooth noted that based solely on the evidence they already had, there was strong reason to believe that one particular woman in Rudy's life had found out about at least one of the others. When the authorities went back to confront that woman, a confession resulted. Your job is to figure out who confessed.

1) Who killed Rudy Marcus?

2) Rudy's personality played a role in his demise, in two distinct ways. Name them.

3) The testimony of two particular people would prove very helpful in bringing the guilty party to justice. Which two?

INSPECTOR FORSOOTH ANSWERS YOUR QUESTIONS

Q1—Is it proven that Mary and Rudy stayed for the whole movie?

They could have left early, but I believe they stayed for the whole thing.

Q2—Since Cornelia was housesitting for Rudy, did she intercept Mary's message on the answering machine?

We have to assume that if Cornelia was in the house, she heard the message, because he had an answering machine, not voice mail.

Q3—Did the gifts have anything to do with the murder?

They sure did, but not in the way you might think.

Q4—Which of the presents Rudy gave was the most valuable?

The emerald brooch was the most valuable, followed by the gold necklace. The red silk scarf was a distant third.

Q5—Was there any perfume scent noticed around the body?
There was a vague scent of perfume around the house, but it wasn't concentrated around the body. Sorry!

Q6—Did the police talk to Mary Stahl's husband?
No, they didn't. Actually, none of the questions asks for two witnesses who might be helpful. I can tell you right now that only one of them is named in the text, so Mr. Stahl is a good guess for the other. Alas, he's not the one.

Q7—How do you know that Daphne only went in the vestibule?
We have to take her word on that. Besides, she was only there a second or two, as Cecily Wheelock could confirm.

Q8—What was Daphne's gift? Was Rudy home when she delivered it?
I don't know what Daphne's gift was, and it really doesn't matter. But I can say that Rudy wasn't home when she delivered it. And his absence turns out to be extremely important in reaching the solution.

Q9—Where in the United States did the murder take place?
Believe it or not, it doesn't really matter. But we can assume from the language in the text that it took place outside of California, and that is important!

Q10—Is the fact that Rudy is an accountant significant?
Yes. He made a living out of reducing people's taxes, including his

own. Income tax, state tax, sales tax—he hated them all. And that, believe it or not, is a big clue.

Q11—Was Cornelia angry at Rudy for not calling her while he was away?
Perhaps, but his failure to do so is good for her in a different sense, which is explained in the solution.

Q12—Where was Rudy when the package was delivered?
Rudy was not home when a particular package was delivered. (I hope that's not misleading!)

CAN YOU SOLVE THE MYSTERY?

Solution on page 260.

WHERE THERE'S A WILL

Marion Webster was one of the most eccentric people ever to walk the planet. To him, communication was a game to be played for personal amusement, and nothing else. And when he died, everyone else was left to explain exactly what had happened. It wasn't easy.

The occasion was the 35th birthday party of Webster's eldest daughter, Laura. Each of his six children was able to make it home for the late-September festivities. Webster had three sons—Eugene, Herbert, and Biff—and three daughters—Laura, Gwen, and Dorothy. All were grown up, but none as yet had started families of their own, a fact that displeased Webster tremendously. As the family patriarch and himself a retired widower, he felt it was his role to push his children in every imaginable way, even if the results didn't always match his expectations. Unfortunately, he used his own will to reward or penalize his children's efforts. It was a fatal mistake.

Instead of simply dividing his estate equally, Webster had designated that each child would receive something consistent with his or her own interests. For example, Herbert, a struggling stockbroker, was to receive the bulk of his father's stock portfolio; Gwen, a budding socialite, was to receive a diamond necklace that had belonged to Webster's own mother. Dorothy, a librarian, was to receive Webster's extensive book collection. And so on.

The birthday weekend was filled with tension. At various times during their brief stay at Webster's Florida retreat, each of the children was summoned into the study to talk about their father's plans to reconfigure his will. The study was an imposing room, with a large oak desk in the middle and three of the four walls taken up by shelves housing his remarkable collection of reference works. It could be said that Webster's children lived in fear of their father. But tension gave way to tragedy early Sunday afternoon, when Marion Webster was found dead at his desk, the victim of a single gunshot wound to the chest.

As is so often the case, Inspector Forsooth wasn't called in until after the initial investigation had failed. One of the reasons for that failure was that none of the six children had much to say about Webster's plans with his will. Said Biff, "Everything that Dad did or said was misinterpreted, unless you knew him awfully well. Me, I was born on April Fool's Day. Maybe I learned early that things aren't always what they seem."

What was known is that the murder occurred in the early afternoon, following lunch. Gwen had made the lunch, and Laura had prepared the dessert. After lunch, Laura, Dorothy, and Herbert were outside by the pool when they heard a shot ring out. They rushed into the study and found nothing except their father's dead body. The other family members then turned up in short order. But if anyone saw anything of great importance, he or she wasn't saying so. As if this weren't frustrating enough, no murder weapon turned up, even though the investigators searched the rest of the house very carefully.

The only real evidence was a piece of paper found on Webster's desk that seemed to shed light on his intentions with his children. But the note contained only cryptic phrases:

I have decided to "rearrange" a portion of my will.

Bond portfolio is satisfactory—generates income.

Plan to decrease Gwen's inheritance will be put on ice.

Herb/pasta salad was commendable, and deserving of
    recognition. But a disappointment after that.

Finally, I've decided that book donations will be limited,
    but funding libraries will increase. (I'm sorry that signs
    got crossed.)

Inspector Forsooth, after getting used to Webster's strange method of communication, was able to solve the case and obtain a confession. He was also able to determine what happened to the murder weapon by concluding that the killer must have returned to the crime scene during a lull in the first, sloppy investigation.

With that in mind, here are your questions:

1) Who killed Marion Webster?

2) Where was the murder weapon hidden after the crime?

3) Which of the children was Webster going to treat harshly in his revised will? (One of them is the killer!)

INSPECTOR FORSOOTH ANSWERS YOUR QUESTIONS

Q1—Why is "rearrange" in quotes?

Because "rear range" is the same thing as "back burner," meaning that some of the will was being left unchanged for now.

Q2—Does the "Herb" in Herb/pasta salad refer to Herbert?

Yes it does.

Q3—Was Webster referring to lunch when he said "a disappointment"? No!

Q4—Was Webster the sort of guy who would change his will over a stupid dessert?

You never know with Webster, but one has to believe that he wasn't that strange.

Q5—Is there a distinction between a stock portfolio and a bond portfolio?

There sure is. The bond portfolio was not going to Herbert the stockbroker.

Q6—Why does Webster's note say "Bond portfolio is satisfactory—generates income"?
Because the name of the person who deserves the income is right there, if you look hard enough.

Q7—What was Eugene to inherit?
I think that question was just answered.

Q8—Is it important that Biff was born on April Fool's Day?
In an incredibly obscure way, yes.

Q9—Did they have pasta salad for lunch?
There is no evidence to suggest that they did.

Q10—Was Herb's childhood commendable?
Apparently it was, and that's what Webster was trying to communicate. As I indicated in my prior answer, whether they actually had pasta salad for lunch is anyone's guess.

Q11—Does "signs" refer to signs of the zodiac?
Yes!

Q12—How many "losers" were there in Webster's revised will?
There were three. And remember, every one of Webster's children is accounted for in his cryptic notes!

Can you solve the mystery?

Solution on page 262.

THE OVERHEAD SMASH

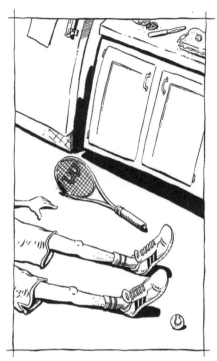

It was no ordinary U. S. Open, that's for sure. This one had a special excitement to it, what with political intrigue in the second week and some breathtaking tennis on the final weekend. But Manny Heitz never made it that far.

Heitz's body was discovered on Friday afternoon during the first week of the tournament. He was working as a linesman throughout the event, and had been scheduled to work two matches on that fateful day—an early-round singles match in the stadium at 11 a.m. and then a late-afternoon doubles match on the grandstand court. But when he didn't show up for the second match, tournament officials sent someone over to his house. Heitz's body was found in the kitchen of his home, not far from the tennis stadium. He was wearing his official U.S. Open outfit.

Heitz had been struck on the head, and the murder weapon wasn't especially difficult to find: his Wilson T2000 tennis racquet lay by his side, the top of its frame stained with blood. Closer examination revealed that there were several strands of hair stuck to the blood, hair that turned out to be Heitz's. The room bore the signs of a struggle, and it was therefore surmised that the death may have been accidental, in the sense that the perpetrator might have struck Heitz without intending to kill him. Either way, the coroner estimated that the time of death was between 12:00 and 2:00 in the afternoon. The autopsy also revealed two separate blows to Heitz's right temple, one of which may have been enough to have knocked him out, the other of which was presumed to have been fatal.

Interviews with other linespeople who worked that first match revealed that no one had any recollection that anything was wrong. However, it turned out that none of them really knew Manny Heitz in any real sense. They were focusing on calling their own lines, and not much else.

Of the people who actually knew the victim, one of the last to see him alive was Ernie Welch, who owned a sporting goods store in the area. Apparently, Heitz had stopped by Welch's store early in the morning on the day of his death to buy a few tennis-related items—wrist bands, a pair of sneakers, and a couple of pairs of socks. Heitz wanted to look his best when he was on the stadium court.

According to Ernie Welch, the match that Heitz was going to be involved with at 11:00 was a big one, as early-rounders go: Tracy Molotov of the Soviet Union versus Chris de la Harpe of South Africa. The match was especially meaningful to Heitz because one of his frequent doubles partners, Wayne Melanson, was Molotov's agent, while another occasional partner, Roger Dant, was de la Harpe's cousin. Each of them had actually tried to bribe Heitz to make calls that were favorable to the player of their choice! At first Heitz thought they were joking, but Welch remembered warning him that he was underestimating their fanaticism.

What happened in the match was truly bizarre. Molotov, the favorite, was beaten by de la Harpe in one of the day's major upsets, in part because the side linesman called Molotov's patented slice serves wide on a couple of crucial break points, thereby taking away one of his most potent weapons. Molotov was absolutely convinced that the balls in question had skidded off the tape, and was livid when the umpire refused to overrule (as they so often decline to do). Molotov eventually lost his cool, and with it the match.

Another friend of the victim, a woman named Janet Stringfellow, had been in the stadium for that match. She later said that the emotions during those line-call arguments were so strained that she joked to a friend, to her later regret, that Heitz would be lucky to escape with his life! But she was on the other side of the court, well up in the stadium, and was unable to see the action very closely. In fact, she said that she had trouble distinguishing the two men who were playing! Apparently the match wasn't nearly as important to Stringfellow as to some of the others. She joked that she hadn't followed the game in a while, and probably wouldn't recognize any tennis players that weren't Jimmy Connors or Björn Borg! She also said that she spent the afternoon at the tournament, trying to reacquaint herself with the whole tennis scene.

Upon investigating Heitz's alleged buddies, Roger Dant and Wayne Melanson, some interesting facts turned up. For one, Melanson was extremely upset by Molotov's early loss, because he thought his client had a chance of breaking through all the way to the semifinals. Melanson didn't see the de la Harpe match personally, but he admitted that early that afternoon, upon finding out about the controversy, he went to Heitz's place to confront him. However, he insisted that by the time he arrived, Heitz was already dead! Melanson left without telling anyone, fearful that someone would suspect his involvement. Investigators noted that Melanson was much bigger than Heitz, and would have had no trouble subduing him.

As for Dant, he said that he had watched the entire Molotov/de la Harpe match, and had then gone to the local public courts and picked up a game. He pointed to his scraped knee, an injury he said he incurred because the courts had not been watered recently and were therefore slippery. Dant also said he had a conversation with a woman who was admiring his "RACQUET" vanity license plate, which was easily visible because of the dark letters on the bright orange background. He said he talked to the woman for over 20 minutes before the pickup game started, and he remembered getting on the court at precisely 1:00 p.m. The authorities, of course, set out to confirm these various claims.

Upon piecing together all these bits of information, Inspector Forsooth was able to come up with the solution—your very next task. Here are the questions you must answer:

1) Who killed Manny Heitz? What was the murder scenario?

2) What was the crucial piece of evidence the killer tried to cover up? Why was his effort doomed to failure?

3) Let's suppose that this case came to trial. Although no one saw the crime committed except for the killer and the victim, name one person whom the prosecution would surely want to get as a witness for its side.

INSPECTOR FORSOOTH ANSWERS YOUR QUESTIONS

Q1—Is Molotov left-handed?

We can deduce that he is, yes, because his "patented slice serves" were called out on "crucial break points" by a "side lines-man." Most break points in tennis arise in the so-called "ad court," where a slice serve is most effective for a left-hander because it brings the ball out wide (à la John McEnroe). However, given that Janet Stringfellow had trouble distinguishing between Molotov and de la Harpe, it follows that both of them are left-handed! (A lot of work for not much reward, wouldn't you say?)

Q2—Don't New York license plates have a white background?
They do now, but they weren't always like that.

Q3—What is the significance of the clothing that the dead man had bought?
Believe it or not, one specific item that Manny Heitz purchased is a big help in tracking down the killer.

Q4—Did Heitz live close to the National Tennis Center?
Hmmm. A good question. Heitz lived about 15 minutes by car from the National Tennis Center in Flushing Meadows, but that's a highly misleading answer!

Q5—The story says that Molotov was from the Soviet Union. Isn't that out-of-date?
No, it is not. And that's a useful clue, in and of itself.

Q6—What is the average length of a men's singles match at the U.S. Open?
It is fairly uncommon for three-out-of-five-set men's matches to take less than two hours, but there is a very good reason why this particular match was shorter than we might be accustomed to. Let's assume each set of the match took one hour. Okay?

Q7—When did New York State adopt its current license plates?
In 1976, the bicentennial year, New York made a patriotic move toward red, white, and blue plates. Prior to that time, the plates were orange with dark blue lettering.

Q8—Was Melanson angry at Heitz? Hadn't Heitz's calls cost Melanson a lot of money?

The answer to the first question is yes: he certainly was angry, at least for a while. The answer to the second question, technically, is no.

Q9—Why in the world was Heitz playing with a T2000? I thought they went out of style years ago!

You're right. They did. The Wilson T2000—the first steel racquet and for years the weapon of choice (so to speak) for one Jimmy Connors—was a revolutionary product but was also one of the worst racquets ever made! However, it was once in vogue.

Q10—Why is the sideline referred to as a "tape"?

Because the match in question was not being played on a hard court, in which case the term "line" would have sufficed.

Q11—Was Heitz wearing the new tennis shoes when he died?

He sure was.

Q12—Did Heitz make it to his 11:00 match?

No. But a sleuth of your skill had figured that out already, right?

CAN YOU SOLVE THE MYSTERY?

Solution on page 263.

PIER FOR THE COURSE

Inspector Forsooth's Final Case (for now) shows how dangerous it is to play with guns—especially when hard-core, aggressive corporate types are involved. The occasion of interest to us is the off-site meeting of the Fairport Firearms Company. For several years the firm's senior and middle managers had met at some unusual locales to bond, try out different management techniques, and ultimately to test the mettle of all those who attended. This time around, the group agreed to go on a hunting and fishing expedition at Lake Nineveh. It was a decision that permanently changed the company and the lives of those who worked for it.

The focus of the weekend was on three of the company's vice presidents, all of whom were extremely hungry for professional advancement: David Willoughby, the chief financial officer; Kevin

Van Allen, the head of the sales division; and Paula Fine, the marketing director. Each of these three was the head of a corporate "team" for the off-site meeting. The reason this turned out to be important is that only the team leaders spent any time by themselves—everyone who worked under them was always in a group, with others to attest to their whereabouts. The three groups took turns occupying different areas of the lakeside, each of which offered its own special terrain. Although no hunting was done per se, everyone had real guns and blanks for use in the role-playing survival games that the teams were engaging in. The whole idea of the weekend was to create a primitive setting that would develop ingenuity and teamwork.

Tragedy struck at lunchtime on the second day of the meeting. Each employee had been given a box lunch containing a peanut-butter-and-jelly sandwich, potato chips, bottled water, and, finally, a caramel apple to celebrate the fall season. The only exception to the rule was senior vice president Wayne Metzger, the second-most-powerful person in the company; he was given a ham sandwich instead of the standby PB&J because of a long-standing and extremely serious allergy to peanut oil. Metzger and company president Bart Strunk were the only two who didn't participate in the management games that morning. Instead, they located themselves on a pier that jutted out into the lake, prepared to enjoy some relaxing trout fishing. But neither one made it off the pier alive.

The first people to reach the crime scene were David Willoughby and his assistant, Sharon Sturgis. In a sense, their appearance was surprising, because just prior to the lunch break Willoughby's group had been out at Rocky Point, the most remote locale of them all. But they wanted to see how the fishing was going—so they headed to the pier They saw the bodies from a distance and ran toward them. Sturgis tried in vain to revive Metzger, who had collapsed for unknown reasons. Willoughby went farther out on the pier, where Bart Strunk lay dead. Strunk had been shot twice in the chest. Willoughby noted to his assistant that the two must have just finished their lunch, as the core of Strunk's caramel apple lay beside him, still white. Metzger's sandwich was finished, but he hadn't gotten to his apple yet. The bottled water, plastic cups, and potato chip bags were strewn around the pier. Clearly the men hadn't had a chance to clean up.

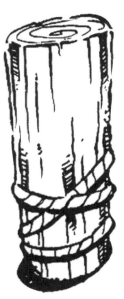

The other two groups—led by Kevin Van Allen and Paula Fine—were quickly called in, and the fun and games stopped right there. Because the woods had been resounding with fake gunfire throughout the day, no one could be sure exactly where the shots that hit Bart Strunk had come from, or, for that matter, when they had been fired. But the murder weapon was eventually fished out of the lake, not far from the pier. Fittingly, Strunk had been shot by one of his firm's own guns.

The search for clues began, and a number of interesting facts turned up. Some had to do with corporate intrigue at Fairport Firearms, such as the fact that Van Allen and Fine had a romantic relationship. They had tried to keep the relationship a secret, but they were caught red-handed on Lake Nineveh: when asked what they were doing during the time just before the discovery of the bodies, they had no choice but to admit that they had sneaked away for a romantic liaison in the woods. The two seemed embarrassed by the disclosure, but they realized that it would have looked much worse if they had been unable to account for their whereabouts. In any event, many people in the company had figured out that Van Allen and Fine had long-term plans for themselves as a couple, plans that included running Fairport Firearms one day.

The odd man out among the three vice presidents was David Willoughby, who had a particularly close working relationship with the late Wayne Metzger. Metzger, as senior vice president, apparently treated Willoughby roughly, and took full use of the corporate power he held. However, Willoughby was also fiercely loyal to Metzger, and always saw to it that Metzger's personal quirks were satisfied. He figured that if Metzger was going to be running the show at some point, it made sense to play along.

As far as the off-site meeting went the murder investigation confirmed some basic details. First of all, because there were so many extra guns around, the murder weapon could not be pinned on any one person or team. However, it was readily determined that the group led by Paula Fine had been in the area closest to the pier for the 20 minutes or so prior to the discovery of the bodies. Sturgis added that as part of standard procedure, she had double-checked Metzger's box lunch after Willoughby's initial check and didn't notice anything wrong with it.

Inspector Forsooth surveyed the evidence and came to a surprising conclusion—that the deaths had resulted from a two-person conspiracy! More than that, there was a twist at the end, because Forsooth claimed that one of the co-conspirators had pulled a double-cross! Your job is to determine who spoiled the fun and games at Lake Nineveh. Specifically, you must answer the following questions:

1) Who killed Bart Strunk?

2) Who killed Wayne Metzger?

3) How was Metzger killed? You must be specific as to how the crime was perpetrated.

INSPECTOR FORSOOTH ANSWERS YOUR QUESTIONS

Q1—Did Metzger collapse because he ate something containing peanut oil?

That's right. It was determined that Metzger died from an allergic reaction that closed his larynx, and traces of peanut oil were found in his stomach.

Q2—Was Metzger poisoned by something in his lunch?

The answer, literally speaking, is no. But he was poisoned, all right. (Note that peanut oil isn't a poison as such, but it is considered a poison in this case, given Metzger's allergy.)

Q3—Did the bottled water or cups play an important role?

The answer is an emphatic yes. The existence of the cups was an essential part of the conspiracy, believe it or not.

Q4—From what distance was Strunk shot?

It simply wouldn't have been possible for anyone to have shot Strunk from afar, because the shots came from an almost head-on angle, eliminating the possibility that the killer had been farther down along the shore. And because of the dense woods, the shots would never have gotten through unless the killer was near the shore.

Q5—Does that mean that someone in the group closest to the pier must have fired the shot?

Absolutely. Remember, though, those groups rotated.

Q6—Which group was scheduled to have been closest to the pier after the lunch break?
Kevin Van Allen's.

Q7—Was it a coincidence that Sharon Sturgis attended to Wayne Metzger?
Not at all. The entire murder plot depended on who took care of which corpse!

Q8—How long does an allergy to peanut oil take to set in?
Not very long. Metzger probably didn't last more than 15 seconds.

Q9—Was it the candied apple that was laced with peanut oil? And did someone know that Metzger was going to eat Strunk's apple?
Believe it or not, the answer to both questions is a resounding yes!

Q10—Was one of the dead guys involved in the conspiracy?
Again, yes!

Q11—Did Willoughby have an alibi?

His alibi was that the apple was still white. Given that he was in a remote locale just prior to when the body was found, it appeared that he couldn't have been involved, because an apple core will turn brown fairly quickly if left out in the open.

Q12—Who died first, Strunk or Metzger?
Great question. The answer is that Strunk died first.

CAN YOU SOLVE THE MYSTERY?

Solution on page 265.

MATCH WITS

WITH

SHERLOCK HOLMES

MEET YOUR COLLEAGUE

Follow the strains of that enigmatic violin, and enter a time warp where you will find your way to Baker Street. Imagine yourself taking tea in front of the fire, served by Mrs. Hudson. You and Dr. Watson can exchange theories as Holmes broods over his violin. Then suddenly, the knock at the door ... the telegram ... the message from Lestrade ... and you're off on a trail to discover the wrongdoer.

Figuring out perplexing puzzles is "elementary" for Sherlock Holmes, but now you have a chance to show off your smarts, too! When you join up with world-famous Sherlock Holmes, his trusty side-kick, Dr. Watson, and the occasional assistance of Inspector Lestrade, you are sure to flush out fiendish felons, uncover nefarious plots, and inevitably cross paths with the dastardly Moriarty.

In order to crack these cases and reveal "whodunit," you'll have to sharpen your wits by breaking codes, sorting out stolen loot, and solving tricky riddles crucial to untangling crimes. Put your powers of deduction to work, and prove that you are smart enough to outwit the cleverest criminals!

CODE ONE

"Take a look at this, Watson," said Holmes as he passed a coded message to his colleague.

The message read:

TO SHERLOCK HOLMES,
T5M5RR5W4W4LLST32LTH3CR5WN
J3W3LSTH4SW4LLB3MYGR32T3STTR46MPH.
                    MORIARTY

"What does it all mean, Holmes?" exclaimed Watson.

"To find that out, Watson, we must break the code. The numbers obviously represent letters."

"But he doesn't use the numbers one or zero, Holmes," said Watson.

"That is simply because they could be mistaken for the letters I and O, Watson," said Holmes as he set about breaking the code.

CAN YOU DECIPHER
THE MESSAGE?

Solution on page 267.

AGE OLD QUESTION

Sherlock Holmes and Dr. Watson had apprehended three men suspected of carrying out the Clapham bank robbery. The three men, Fish, Giles, and Hill, were taken to Scotland Yard, where they were interviewed by Inspector Lestrade. As Lestrade noted down the age of each of the men, he was aware that if he reversed each of the digits of their ages, all three men would still remain the same age. Lestrade also noticed that Fish was only a third the age of Giles, who in turn was twice the age of Hill. The combined age of all three men was 121 years.

HOW OLD WAS EACH OF THE THREE MEN?

Solution on page 267.

SPENDING SPREE

While wearing one of his famous disguises, Sherlock Holmes followed a suspect through London's busy streets. The suspect entered two shops. In order not to look suspicious, Holmes purchased an item in each of the shops. In the first shop Holmes spent one-fourth of all his money, and in the second shop he spent one-fourth of what remained.

IF HOLMES SPENT £21 IN TOTAL,
HOW MUCH DID HE HAVE TO BEGIN WITH?

Solution on page 267.

LESTRADE IN STRIDE

Sherlock Holmes and Dr. Watson had been spectators at the annual Scotland Yard athletics meeting. Inspector Lestrade had done extremely well for his team. He was the first in two events and second in another. Lestrade's team had scored a total of 25 points, making them outright winners of the whole meeting. In each event points were awarded for first, second, and third place. Lestrade's team had gained their points by winning four events, coming in second in two and taking a third place in another.

HOW MANY POINTS DID INSPECTOR LESTRADE SCORE FOR HIS TEAM?

Solution on page 267.

ASTON AVENUE ROBBERIES

Aston Avenue was a private row of only five houses numbered 1, 2, 3, 4, and 5. The owners of these houses were Messrs. Jones, White, Smith, Green, and Brown. All five houses had recently been robbed, and Sherlock Holmes called to speak with each of the owners. Unfortunately, all five were not at home. Holmes spoke with a passerby and was able to record the following facts:

1. Jones lived two doors to the left of Smith.
2. Brown and Green lived on his right.
3. Both White and Brown lived in an even-numbered house.

FROM THE ABOVE, CAN YOU DETERMINE IN WHICH HOUSE ON ASTON AVENUE MR. GREEN LIVED?

Solution on page 267.

A THREATENING GIFT

Sherlock Holmes had received two telegrams from the infamous Professor Moriarty within a space of 3 hours. The first was a threat against the famous detective's life, while the second said that he, the professor, had organized a present for Holmes. The remainder of the second telegram contained the following riddle:

> He who makes it, makes it to sell,
> He who buys it, does not use it,
> He who uses it, does not know it.

Watson read both telegrams. "It doesn't make sense to me, Holmes," said Watson. "First he threatens your life and then he organizes a present for you."

"Solve the riddle, Watson. Then you'll see that it makes sense," replied Holmes.

WHAT WAS IT THAT MORIARTY INTENDED TO SEND HOLMES?

Solution on page 267.

IDENTIFY THE WITNESSES

Sherlock Holmes was questioning three men who had been witness to a murder, Messrs. Franks, Richards, and Andrews. By coincidence, their first names were Richard, Frank, and Andrew. Holmes remarked to Mr. Richards on this.

"Yes, I noticed that as well," he replied. "But none of us has the first name that matches our surname. My first name happens to be Andrew."

CAN YOU GIVE THE FULL NAME OF ALL THREE WITNESSES?

Solution on page 267.

STAKE OUT THE PROFESSOR

Sherlock Holmes sat by the fire at 221b Baker Street, studying some information on a note.

"What's that you're reading, Holmes?" asked Watson.

"It's a list of houses on Fitzroy Street that have all been robbed in the last six days by Professor Moriarty."

Watson glanced at the list, which read:

MONDAY	NO. 4
TUESDAY	NO. 16
WEDNESDAY	NO. 12
THURSDAY	NO. 3
FRIDAY	NO. 7
SATURDAY	NO. 28

"Great Scott!" exclaimed Watson. "And today's Sunday. He'll probably strike again tonight."

"He will, Watson," replied Holmes. "But this time we'll be waiting inside the house for him."

WHICH HOUSE ON FITZROY STREET WILL MORIARTY ROB NEXT?

Solution on page 267.

IF THE COAT FITS ...

Sherlock Holmes, Dr. Watson, and Inspector Lestrade were enjoying a cup of tea in the study of 221b Baker Street, when they were called away on an urgent matter. Each grabbed an overcoat and rushed from the house. It turned out that all three had grabbed the wrong overcoat.

"This coat is much too tight on me," remarked Lestrade to the person wearing Watson's coat.

WHOSE OVERCOAT
WAS EACH OF THEM WEARING?

*Solution
on page 268.*

THE BUTLER DID IT

Sherlock Holmes arrested the butler of the Westwood mansion for poisoning the entire Westwood family. After confessing, the butler went on to explain to Holmes just exactly how it was done. He filled a wineglass half full of wine, and another glass twice the size one-third full of wine. He then topped up each glass with poison before pouring the contents of both glasses into an empty wine decanter.

CAN YOU DEDUCE
HOW MUCH
OF THE MIXTURE
IS WINE AND
HOW MUCH
IS POISON?

*Solution on
page 268.*

IN TRAINING

To pass the time while traveling on a long train journey, Sherlock Holmes sent his colleague, Dr. Watson, a little teaser to work out. See the diagram below:

7			= 19
		5	= 16
	3		= 10

‖   ‖   ‖   ⟍⟍
15   16   14   ⟋17

"What do you want me to do with this, Holmes?" asked Watson. "Simple, my dear Watson. Insert the following numbers in their proper place so that each column adds up to the number indicated. The missing numbers are: 4, 6, 1, 2, 8, 9."

By the time their train journey had ended, Watson had failed to complete the teaser correctly.

CAN YOU DO BETTER?

Solution on page 268.

WHICH WAY DID HE GO?

Sherlock Holmes and Dr. Watson were running after a criminal in a crowded London street. They turned a corner only to find that the criminal was nowhere to be seen. Holmes turned to a beggar sitting at the side of the road. "Did you happen to see a man wearing a tall black hat and a cape pass this way?"

"Yes," replied the beggar.

"Which direction did he take?" asked Watson.

"Well, when I first saw him he was facing due east, but then he did a right turn, before taking a left turn and heading off in that direction."

WHICH WAY DID THE CRIMINAL GO?

Solution on page 268.

AN UPSTANDING VICTIM

A murderer had weighted down the body of his victim and dumped him in the Thames. Unknown to the murderer, the point where he dumped the body was much shallower than he had thought. Sherlock Holmes was called to the scene, where he discovered that the body was standing upright in the water. One-fourth of the victim was buried in the mud, five-eighths of the body was covered by water, and the remaining 9½ inches protruded from the water.

CAN YOU DETERMINE THE HEIGHT OF THE VICTIM
IN FEET AND INCHES?

Solution on page 268.

REPORTING A CRIME

Sherlock Holmes, Dr. Watson, and Inspector Lestrade were all involved in the solving of a recent murder. The day after the case was concluded, all three wrote individual reports on the crime. The combined number of pages written was 99. Lestrade wrote 5 more pages than Holmes, who in turn had submitted 17 more pages than Watson.

How many pages did each of them write?

Solution on page 268.

TRAPPED!

Professor Moriarty had trapped Holmes and Watson in a room with no windows and only one door. After a few minutes, they could hear the sound of a pump starting up, and within moments the room began to fill with water. "Great Scott, we're going to drown!" shouted Watson.

Holmes moved over to the door, where he found it to be secured by a combination lock. There was a note pinned to the door in Moriarty's handwriting. The note revealed that the combination lock contained six numbers. The sum of the first two numbers was 69. The next two totalled 79, and the last two 29. At this point Holmes remembered something that Moriarty had said as he had closed them in the room. "It will help you, Holmes, if you remember that the difference between the first and second, the third and fourth, and the fifth and sixth is 13 in each case!" Holmes smiled as he set to work on the combination lock.

CAN YOU FIND THE SIX NUMBERS THAT WOULD OPEN THE DOOR AND RELEASE HOLMES AND WATSON?

Solution on page 268.

GOING OFF IN ALL DIRECTIONS

Sherlock Holmes, Dr. Watson and Inspector Lestrade shared a cab to Euston Station, where they would each catch a train to separate destinations.

1. Holmes would not be taking the train to Brighton.
2. Watson wasn't taking the train to Manchester.
3. Lestrade wasn't taking the Edinburgh train.
4. The Brighton train left before Watson's train.

FROM THE ABOVE INFORMATION, CAN YOU DISCOVER THE INTENDED DESTINATIONS OF ALL THREE?

Solution on page 269.

KILLER IN THE CLUB

Sherlock Holmes received an urgent telegram from a client. The client felt certain that his life was in danger. Holmes and Watson hurried to his lodgings only to find that they were too late. The man had been murdered minutes before they arrived.

"I found him lying there," said the landlady. "Before he died he muttered something about belonging to a secret club and quoted the number 92."

"Damned strange thing to say, Holmes," said Watson.

Holmes nodded in agreement. "Did he say anything else?" Holmes asked the landlady.

"I asked him who had done this terrible thing to him, but he just repeated the number 92!" she answered.

Holmes thanked her for her help and discharged her. He then proceeded to search the dead man's room. He came across a letter addressed to the man that was from the other three members of the secret club. Their names were Mr. Wilson, Mr. Updike, and

Mr. Brown. In the top left of the letter was the name of the dead man, Mr. Smith (Code 69). From this, Holmes deduced that he had been murdered by another member of the club, and that the number that he had uttered to the landlady was in fact the code number of the murderer.

HOLMES WAS THEN QUICKLY ABLE TO SUPPLY
THE NAME OF THE KILLER. CAN YOU?

Solution on page 269.

RIDDLE ME THIS . . .

Holmes glanced at a note that had been slipped under the door of 221b Baker Street.

"What is it, Holmes?" asked Watson, seeing the concern on the face of his colleague.

"It's a note from Moriarty. He intends to kidnap a prominent member of Parliament, and he has sent us a riddle as to the identity of the victim."

The riddle read:

GREAT WISE OLD MAN, AT WILL

WHOM DID MORIARTY INTEND TO KIDNAP?

Solution on page 269.

ONE MEASLY DIAMOND

Moriarty and his two partners in crime, Fingers and Porky, sat looking at the diamonds piled on the table in front of them. There was a knock at the door, which Porky answered. Mr. X, the brains behind the robbery, entered. Moriarty sent Porky to check the surrounding area to make sure that Mr. X had not been followed. Mr. X then took Porky's seat at the table. They sat in silence for several moments, until Moriarty bent forward and took half the diamonds plus one from the pile. Mr. X then took two-thirds of what remained, placed them in his pocket and, without a word, left the building. Fingers then took two-thirds of what remained and placed them in a bag. He smiled at Moriarty and took one more diamond, which he quickly shoved into the top pocket of his coat.

When Porky returned, he glanced down at the solitary diamond lying on the table.

"Is this all I get, one measly diamond?" he grunted.

HOW MANY DIAMONDS HAD ORIGINALLY BEEN ON THE TABLE?

Solution on page 269.

WHO RODE TINKERBELL?

Lord Knight invited Sherlock Holmes, Dr. Watson, and Inspector Lestrade to spend the weekend at his country estate. After showing the excellent stable facilities, Lord Knight suggested that they, along with the stables' head boy, Martin, should all take part in a horse race around the boundaries of the estate. Everybody readily agreed.

The last horse to finish was Fair Sensation. Ivory Tower finished first. Watson rode Kestrel. Lestrade's horse finished fourth. Holmes didn't finish second. Lord Knight finished three places behind Spring Goddess.

FROM THE ABOVE INFORMATION, CAN YOU IDENTIFY:

1. Who rode Tinkerbell?
2. Which horse Martin rode?

Solution on page 269.

FIVE IN A ROW

Sherlock Holmes, Dr. Watson, and Mrs. Hudson left Baker Street to spend an evening at the theatre. In the foyer, they met Inspector Lestrade and Sergeant Baxter. All five had a drink in the theatre bar before taking their seats to enjoy the performance. All five sat in the same row together, taking up the seats numbered 35, 36, 37, 38, and 39.

FROM THE INFORMATION BELOW, CAN YOU IDENTIFY THE SEATS OCCUPIED BY INSPECTOR LESTRADE AND SERGEANT BAXTER?

1. Watson sat to the left of Holmes, but not directly.

2. Sergeant Baxter sat in an odd-numbered seat with Holmes directly on his right.

3. Mrs. Hudson sat to the left of Lestrade, but not directly.

Solution on page 269.

DINNER AT LADY MCBRIDE'S

Dr. Watson, who had been keeping an eye on events at Lady McBride's dinner party, reported back to Sherlock Holmes at 221b Baker Street.

"I need to know the arrival times of the guests, Watson," said Holmes.

Watson glanced at his notepad. "Yes, here it is. The arrival times are as follows," said Watson. "7:30, 7:45, 7:50, 7:59, 8:05, with the last guest arriving at 8:20."

"Very good, Watson," said Holmes. "But I need to know just exactly which guest arrived at which time."

"Oh," said Watson, somewhat embarrassed. "I didn't write that down, Holmes."

Eventually Watson was able to pass the following information to Holmes:

1. Lady Barclay, who wasn't the first to arrive, arrived before Lord Hadden.

2. Sir Harry Trump arrived 15 minutes after Lord Winterbottom.

3. It was one of the ladies who arrived 6 minutes after Sir John Penn.

4. Lady James arrived 15 minutes before Lord Hadden.

CAN YOU DEDUCE THE EXACT ARRIVAL TIME OF EACH OF THE SIX GUESTS?

Solution on page 269.

ON THE BRIGHTON TRAIN

Sherlock Holmes was traveling by train from London to Brighton. Five other gentlemen shared the compartment with him. They were Messrs. Andrews, Baker, Clark, Dawson, and Easton. It turned out that each of these gentlemen lived on a London street that bore the name of one of the others.

FROM THE FOLLOWING INFORMATION, CAN YOU MATCH UP EACH OF THE FIVE MEN WITH THE STREET WHERE HE LIVED?

1. Mr. Andrews sat between Sherlock Holmes and the other gentleman who lived on Baker Street.

2. Mr. Baker, who sat opposite Mr. Dawson, had the gentleman who lived on Clark Street sitting next to him.

3. The gentleman opposite Holmes lived on Easton Street.

Solution on page 269.

MISS ALDRIDGE'S BOARDERS

Miss Aldridge, who ran a large boarding house in Acton town, had sent a telegram to Sherlock Holmes requesting his help on a matter of great importance. Within an hour of receiving the telegram, Holmes and his assistant, Dr. Watson, arrived at the large house on Acton High Street.

"I'm quite concerned," said Miss Aldridge as she led them into the parlor. "I'm positive that one of my guests is trying to poison me."

"How many guests do you have?" asked Watson as he sat down in front of the roaring fire.

"Quite a few," replied the old

lady. "Half of them are salesmen, a quarter of them teach at the local college, and one-seventh are shop owners. There are also three widowed ladies, but I don't suspect any of them."

FROM THE ABOVE INFORMATION, CAN YOU FIGURE OUT HOW MANY GUESTS LIVED AT THE BOARDING HOUSE?

Solution on page 270.

HE SAID, SHE SAID

"I'm puzzled," said Lady Ashton to Sherlock Holmes. "One of my four servants has stolen my gold bracelet. I've questioned each of them, but I'm still none the wiser. Branson, the butler, said that Smythe, the gardener, did it, while Mary, the maid, said Smythe told her that Branson did it. Smythe told me Branson did it, and Wilson, the handyman, said he knew which one was the thief but he did not wish to say." Lady Ashton sighed, then continued, "I've known Branson and Smythe for many years and I've never known either of them to tell the truth."

Sherlock Holmes smiled as he filled his pipe. "Assuming that the butler and the gardener have not changed their ways, and that Mary and Wilson are telling the truth, it is quite a simple task to deduce which of them is the thief," said Holmes.

CAN YOU WORK OUT WHICH ONE OF THE STAFF STOLE THE BRACELET?

Solution on page 270.

MEMBERS OF THE COMMITTEE

Sherlock Holmes and Dr. Watson were enjoying a quiet drink in the members' lounge of the Criminologists' Club when four men entered by way of the private office. "Ah, here come the four new committee members," announced Holmes.

"I don't recognize any of them," said Watson.

"Before you stand the chairman, vice-chairman, treasurer, and secretary," replied Holmes. "Their surnames are Hopkins, Smythe, White, and Knight."

Holmes then went on to explain that the treasurer and the chairman were cousins, that Hopkins and Smythe were not related to each other, that the vice-chairman's wife was a well-known actress, and the secretary was engaged to Lord Winterbottom's daughter.

He also pointed out that White and the treasurer were not on speaking terms, and that Hopkins and White were the only ones who were married.

CAN YOU IDENTIFY EACH COMMITTEE MEMBER'S NEW POSITION WITHIN THE CLUB?

Solution on page 270.

FOUR INTO SIXTEEN

"I'm bored," said Dr. Watson to Sherlock Holmes. "This train journey seems to be going on forever."

Sherlock Holmes smiled at his companion and took a sheet of paper from his coat pocket. On the sheet of paper Holmes drew a large square. He then divided this square into sixteen squares (see diagram). He then took four coins from his pocket and asked Watson to place each coin on one of the squares in such a way that no two coins ended up in the same row either horizontally, vertically or diagonally.

Can you achieve this?
(There are several possible solutions.)

Solution on page 270.

BACKWATER'S END

"It was undoubtedly one of the staff who murdered Lord Backwater," said Sherlock Holmes to Dr. Watson. "Have you interviewed them?"

"Yes," replied Watson, glancing at his notes. "It turns out that the maid is the sister of the butler's granddaughter, who, in turn, is the gardener's brother's mother."

FROM THE ABOVE INFORMATION, CAN YOU TELL
HOW THE GARDENER AND THE BUTLER WERE RELATED?

Solution on page 270.

A SCION IN DANGER

When Lady Sharp reported the kidnapping of her young son to Sherlock Holmes, Holmes knew that the crime could only have been carried out by one man—Professor Moriarty.

Lady Sharp produced a ransom note for £10,000. The note also carried a warning that should the money not be paid, she would never see her son alive again. As Lady Sharp left 221b Baker Street, a note was delivered by hand to Sherlock Holmes. "Blast!" cried Holmes as he read the note before passing it to Dr. Watson. "Moriarty knows that we are on the case, Watson. We must act quickly if we are to save the life of Lady Sharp's son!"

Watson read the note. "I don't understand, Holmes. This note is nothing more than gobbledegook!"

"Not so, Watson," cried Holmes as he grabbed his coat. "Unless we find Moriarty's hiding place quickly, we will be too late to find Lady Sharp's son alive!"

The note read:
HATED HALLS TEAK STREAM HARPS TOADY!

CAN YOU DECIPHER THE NOTE?

Solution on page 270.

WHO DID WHAT?

Sherlock Holmes sat opposite Inspector Lestrade in Lestrade's office at Scotland Yard. Sergeant Smith entered with three prisoners, who were stood in a line in front of Lestrade's desk. Holmes watched with interest as Lestrade interrogated the three men.

Barnett stood between the man who was clean-shaven and the man who had stolen a cigar case. Black, who had stolen the wallet, had been arrested at the same time as Wetherby. It was the man with the mustache, not the one with the beard, who had stolen the gold watch.

CAN YOU IDENTIFY EACH OF THE MEN, MATCHING THEM TO:

1. The item each had stolen, and

2. Whether each was clean-shaven or had a mustache or a beard?

Solution on page 271.

MORIARTY'S HAUL

During the course of one night Professor Moriarty robbed five jewellers, taking only diamonds from each one. During his investigation, Sherlock Holmes discovered that one jeweller had lost ¼ of the total diamonds stolen, another had lost ⅓, a third had lost ⅙, the fourth had lost ¹⁄₁₂, and the last jeweller had lost a total of 22 diamonds.

HOW MANY DIAMONDS HAD BEEN STOLEN ALTOGETHER?

Solution on page 271.

FORGE ON!

Sherlock Holmes and Dr. Watson had followed two counterfeiters to their secret printing place. They waited outside for quite some time before bursting in and taking the two men by surprise. Next to the printing press they found some £5,000 in forged bills. Holmes then asked the two men to empty out their pockets. Thereupon Holmes recovered £227 more in forged bills.

IF ONE FORGER HAD £35 MORE THAN THE OTHER,
HOW MUCH DID EACH OF THEM HAVE IN HIS POCKET?

Solution on page 271.

MINT CONDITION

Sherlock Holmes and Dr. Watson were called to the Royal Mint, where they were informed by an executive that there was at least one thief in the building. Over a period of several days, a large number of gold coins had disappeared. Holmes decided to set a trap. He placed a box containing a number of gold coins in an area where it was easily accessible to everybody in the building. He and Watson then hid themselves behind some large cabinets to observe the scene. After a few minutes, a man appeared, looked

inside the box, and removed a third of the coins. Only seconds later, the man returned and removed a third of what remained. Some 10 minutes later, another man appeared and he proceeded to remove a third of what remained. Holmes then checked the box to find that only eight gold coins remained.

HOW MANY GOLD COINS HAD ORIGINALLY BEEN
IN THE BOX?

Solution on page 271.

WELL-ARMED

Professor Moriarty was about to carry out a daring robbery with two other criminals, Stoneface Murphy and Fingers Malloy. In order that none of them would be recognized, they each wore a false beard. They were also armed. One carried a rifle, another a pistol, and the third a club. Moriarty entered the bank behind the one who wore the false brown beard and in front of the one who carried the club. Fingers had used the pistol in a previous robbery and was disappointed that he didn't have it on this occasion. It was the one with the false red beard who carried the club.

IF FINGERS DID NOT
WEAR THE FALSE
BROWN BEARD,
WHO CARRIED
THE CLUB?

Solution on page 271.

A SHOT RANG OUT

Sherlock Holmes studied the dead victim who lay on the library floor. Dr. Watson entered the room. "I've spoken with the maid and she is quite adamant that she heard the shot ring out at 12:15 p.m., Holmes," he announced, "which completely destroys your theory that the deed took place some time earlier."

"I still feel she is mistaken, Watson," said Holmes with some confidence.

"I doubt it, Holmes," replied Watson. "She was dusting in the study when she heard the shot. She remembers standing bolt upright at the sound of the blast and she remembers looking directly into the mirror and seeing the clock behind her. It was unmistakably 12:15 p.m."

Holmes smiled at his colleague, "Then I was correct all along, Watson," he exclaimed.

WHAT TIME DID
THE MAID ACTUALLY
HEAR THE SHOT?

Solution on page 271.

NOT QUITE CRICKET

Sherlock Holmes, Dr. Watson, Inspector Lestrade, and Sergeant Smith were all playing for the Scotland Yard select cricket team in a charity match. While in the locker room getting ready for the match, each of the four accidentally put on a jersey belonging to one of the others.

FROM THE FOLLOWING INFORMATION, CAN YOU
FIGURE OUT WHOSE JERSEY EACH OF THEM WAS WEARING?

1. Watson wasn't wearing the jersey that belonged to Lestrade.
2. Holmes didn't wear Watson's jersey nor vice versa.
3. Sergeant Smith went to bat ahead of the person wearing Watson's jersey.

Solution on page 271.

THEY HAD IT COVERED

While working on a murder case, Sherlock Holmes, Dr. Watson, and Inspector Lestrade found themselves searching a desolate Yorkshire moor for the murder weapon. During the search, they were assisted by a police sergeant and a constable. Before the weapon was found, every one of them had covered a lot of ground in his search.

FROM THE FOLLOWING INFORMATION,
CAN YOU DEDUCE JUST EXACTLY HOW MUCH GROUND
WAS COVERED BY INSPECTOR LESTRADE?

1. Holmes, Watson, and the constable had covered 9 miles between them.

2. Lestrade, Watson, and the sergeant covered 16 miles.

3. Watson, Holmes, and Lestrade covered 12 miles, while the total number of miles covered by Lestrade and the constable was 7.

Solution on page 271.

CAUGHT RED-HANDED

Professor Moriarty and three of his criminal colleagues rushed from a hardware shop, each carrying a handful of money which he had stolen from the poor owner. In total they had £94. Moriarty had £13 more than Bloggs, who in turn had £5 less than Norris, while Hunt had £3 more than Moriarty.

CAN YOU DEDUCE HOW MUCH EACH OF THE FOUR CARRIED INDIVIDUALLY?

Solution on page 271.

MORIARTY IN TOP SECURITY

As a result of excellent work by Sherlock Holmes, the infamous Professor Moriarty was being held in the special security wing of Wormwood Scrubs Prison. In all, there were twelve cells in the special wing, four on each landing (see diagram below):

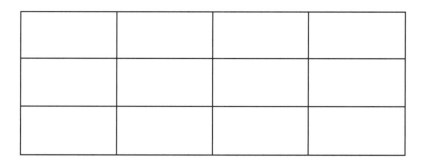

FROM THE FOLLOWING INFORMATION, CAN YOU PLACE EACH PRISONER IN HIS PROPER CELL?

1. Little's cell was on the landing directly below the landing where Robb and Gunn had their cells.

2. Pearce's cell was directly above Conn's cell, who was on the landing above the landing where Hobbs and Webb had their cells.

3. Field had his cell directly to the right of Webb's cell and was directly below the cell occupied by Robb.

4. Tibbs had his cell directly to the left of Milne's cell, which was directly above Moriarty's.

5. Kidd's cell was directly to the left of the cell occupied by Pearce.

6. Moriarty was in the cell directly above the cell occupied by Webb.

7. Hobbs' cell was directly below Gunn's cell.

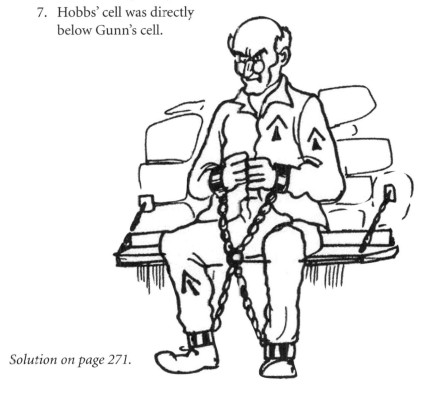

Solution on page 271.

FOILED AGAIN!

While serving a prison sentence in Wormwood Scrubs Prison, Professor Moriarty made five separate escape attempts on each day from Monday to Friday. On each attempt, he tried a different method: a) Disguised as a prison officer. b) Tried to tunnel from his cell. c) Attempted to bribe a prison officer. d) Exchanged identity with a visitor. e) Attempted to sneak out with a work party.

FROM THE FOLLOWING INFORMATION, CAN YOU DETERMINE WHICH METHOD WAS USED ON WHICH DAY?

1. Moriarty attempted to escape disguised as a prison officer two days before his attempted bribe of a prison officer.

2. He tried to tunnel out of his cell the day after his attempt disguised as a prison officer.

3. His attempt to sneak out with the work party didn't take place on Monday or Friday.

4. Moriarty exchanged identity with a visitor the day after his attempt to join the work party.

Solution on page 272.

MYSTERY CRATE

In a warehouse, Sherlock Holmes came across some crates set out in a triangle (see diagram). All the crates (apart from the one at the head of the triangle) were numbered.

CAN YOU DEDUCE THE NUMBER OF THE LAST CRATE?

8	5	4	3
13	9	7	
22	16		
?			

Solution on page 272.

SOMETHING'S FISHY

While spending a weekend fishing in the country, Sherlock Holmes and Dr. Watson were asked to investigate a series of robberies that had taken place at three cottages which were situated close to the fishing lodge where they were staying.

FROM THE FOLLOWING INFORMATION, CAN YOU NAME
THE FAMILY THAT LIVED AT EACH COTTAGE AND
THE ITEM THEY HAD HAD STOLEN BY THE ROBBERS?

1. The Madisons didn't live at No. 3, nor did they lose a gold watch.
2. The O'Connors didn't live at No. 5.
3. £50 was stolen from No. 3.
4. The Newtons didn't live at No. 1, where a crystal decanter was stolen.

Solution on page 272.

SOLUTIONS

SHERMAN OLIVER HOLMES

The Missing Monet (page 5)—"All three suspects had receptacles that could hold a rolled-up painting." Sherman was doing his best to make his Alabama-born accent sound British. "The messenger had a document tube, old boy. The uncle had a cane. The woman had an umbrella. And while it's tempting to accuse the last person to walk through the reception area, that wouldn't be cricket. The painting could have been cut out of its frame at any time and no one may have noticed."

Wilson snickered. "So it could be any of them."

"And it could be an employee who found someplace clever to hide the painting. But only one suspect arrived limping on one leg and departed limping on the other. I think if you examine the older gentleman's cane you'll find that it's hollow."

"You may be right," the sergeant said. "We'll check it out. But let me fill you in on something, old boy. You're no relation to Sherlock Holmes. Sherlock Holmes was fictional."

Sherman laughed. "Nonsense. Why would Dr. Watson make up those stories if they weren't true?"

"Because Dr. Watson was also fict . . . Oh, forget it."

A Maze of Suspects (page 8)—The audience of five

squirmed in the narrow corner of the hedge until they were all facing the strange little man with the funny accent. "Two of your stories agree on one point. The electricity was turned off—from shortly after Mr. and Mrs. Turner's arrival until after the murder."

The highway patrolman laughed. "It doesn't take a Sherlock Holmes to figure that out."

"Sherman Holmes," the little man corrected the patrolman. "And as I said, the solution is elementary. Since the fountain in the center of the maze works by electricity, it couldn't have been running at the time of the murder, as Mr. McQuire testified. Of course, Mr. McQuire didn't know the fountain was off, because he was somewhere else at the time—robbing and killing Kyle Turner, I presume.

Bus Station Bomber (page 11)—The two cab drivers, the

clerk, and the bomb squad officer all gaped in disbelief.

Sergeant Wilson tried to look nonchalant. "I caught the clue, too," he lied. "But I'll let you have the fun of telling them."

"Thanks," Sherman said, playing along. "If the perpetrator had picked a more complex bomb, it wouldn't have been so easy."

"But that's what makes it hard," the bomb squad officer objected. "You can buy a wind-up clock just about anywhere. And as for the sticks of dynamite . . . "

"Let's stick with the clock," interrupted Sherman. "The alarm hand is what set off the explosives, correct?"

"Correct."

"So, let's say it's two p.m. and I set the alarm for three. When will the bomb go off? At three a.m.—or at three p.m. the next day?"

"At three a.m., of course, an hour later."

"Then how do you explain the fact that the bomb didn't go off until thirteen hours after the witness saw it placed inside the locker?"

The bomb expert scratched his head. "I can't explain it."

"That's right," Sherman said. "There's no way to explain it, except to say that the night clerk is lying. He planted the bomb himself—at some time after three a.m."

The Postman Rings Once (page 14)—"If it wasn't suicide," said Thomas, "then any one of us could have killed him. No one has a good alibi."

"True," Wilson agreed and turned to Sherman Holmes.

"True," Sherman agreed. "But . . . " And he raised a pudgy finger. "Only one of you lied about when you checked the mail." He lowered the finger, pointing it at Nigel Liggit. "You, Nigel, actually entered the front hall between 2:30 and 2:50. You steamed open the letter and read its frightening contents. You got rid of the letter—a bad job, I must say—then loaded your uncle's gun and tracked him down."

"Bravo," Nigel said with a sneer. "But you could make up a similar story about either one of my brothers."

Sherman smiled. "Let's see Thomas's letter from that bill collector." Thomas pulled it from his pocket and handed it over.

"Notice the shoe print?"

"That's mine," said Gerald, "from when I came in and stepped on the mail."

"And the water ring? Where did that come from?"

"Not from me," said Thomas. "My hands were full of luggage. I went right upstairs and unpacked."

Sherman turned to face Nigel and his incriminating martini. "When you checked the mail, you put your glass on top of Thomas's letter. That means you didn't check it at three p.m., but earlier—between the time of Gerald's shoe print and Thomas's removal of the bill collector's letter."

Foul Ball Burglary (page 17)—"Excuse me," a high-pitched voice drawled. "I can tell you who stole the coins—if you're interested."

The startled officers turned to see a dapper little man step out from behind the leafy palm fronds. "Who are you?" the tall one demanded.

"Sherman Holmes, at your service. The thief was Jake."

"Jake?" The tall officer had to think for a second. "You mean the kid who discovered the robbery? How could he be the robber?"

Sherman knew he had their attention. He took his time, reaching into his coat pocket and pulling out a briar pipe.

"What young Jake discovered," Sherman said as he sucked on the unlit pipe, "was a broken window, a screeching burglar alarm, and a coin collection lying temptingly on the table. All he had to do was yell back that there'd been a robbery. Then, while the rest of us went around to the front of the house, Jake slipped inside, turned over the table, and took the coins. They may be in his pockets or he may have hidden them somewhere. But Jake's your thief."

The tall officer still looked interested. "Can you prove what you just said?"

"Of course, old bean," Sherman said, insulted at the notion that he would form a theory without proof. "Go back to the crime scene and check the broken window glass. It's underneath the tablecloth. That means the table was overturned after the baseball broke the window, not before. It couldn't be anyone but Jake."

The Unsafe Safe House (page 20)—"The name is Sherman Holmes, private investigator." He took a deep breath, then turned to the rookie. "Please arrest Captain Loeb."

"What?" Loeb was instantly furious. "That's garbage. I'll have your P.I. license revoked so fast . . . "

For once Sherman was glad he didn't have a license. "Ask the captain how he could have arrived without a coat and yet was planning to leave with one. And don't let him say it's not his coat. His notepad was in the pocket."

The rookie's hand shook as he pulled his service revolver. "Are you sure, mister?"

"I am," Sherman replied. "I've been staring at that bloody trench coat for an hour. Frankie would naturally open the door to the captain in charge of his case. Loeb took off his coat, made himself comfortable, then strangled Frankie with his belt. It was only after leaving the house, with the front door locked behind him, that the captain realized he'd left his coat inside."

The Crystal Vanishes (page 23)—"The crystal didn't abandon you," Sherman said. "It's just playing a little joke." He had to handle this delicately. The last thing he wanted was to put an end to these weekly events, something that would surely happen if one of his spirit-loving friends were exposed as a thief.

"If memory serves, Luther freshened our coffee just a few minutes ago. And yet the coffee carafe still seems to be full." Sherman carried the glass carafe into the kitchen and carefully emptied the contents into the sink. Sitting there in the bottom of the carafe was the crystal ball. "You see? It dematerialized from the box and rematerialized here."

Agatha and Grimelda laughed with relief. So did Luther, although Sherman caught his eye and gave him a serious, warning glance, letting Luther know that he knew the truth. While clearing the table, Luther had sneaked the crystal out of the box and into the carafe. As the host, he could have easily recovered it after the others had left.

The Pointing Corpse (page 25)—Sergeant Wilson scratched his head. "There's no way you can know what he was pointing at."

"Oh, yes, there is," Sherman said. "His battery's dead."

"So what?"

"So, a dead battery probably means his lights were on." Sherman checked the dashboard and saw that he was right. "Let's say Mervin had a rendezvous here last night with someone from the Charity Board, perhaps to get information for his story. That person realized Mervin was getting too close to the truth and killed him. But before dying, Mervin saw something . . . "

"Yeah, yeah," Wilson growled. "And he pointed to it. But which of the three things was he pointing at?"

"It was night, remember? The lake and trees would have been invisible in the dark, especially with all the cloud cover we've had lately. The one visible thing would have been that glowing neon sign. That's what Mervin meant. The killer was Arthur Curtis."

Bell, Booke, or Kendall? (page 28)—"It was the intern," Wilson guessed.

Sherman looked surprised. "No, of course not. There was no thief."

"Sure there was. Mr. Boren told us . . . " The sergeant's eyes widened. "Oh!"

"Precisely. I don't know why Arvin Boren wanted to kill his vice president, but it had nothing to do with stolen plans. He killed Silver in the copy room, then he found a witness and 'discovered' the body. Boren made up that story about Silver trying to catch the thief and, of course, Silver wasn't around to contradict him."

"What made you suspect Boren?"

"I suspected from the beginning, but I had no proof. So I made up a story about the plans having to be in the mail chute. Boren needed to preserve the illusion of a thief, so he grabbed a set of plans and tossed them down the chute. That's the only way to explain why the plans are on top of the yellow envelopes instead of underneath them."

The Wayward Will (page 30)—Sherman edged his considerable bulk between Harmon Grove and the briefcase. Then, like a quarterback, he tucked the leather briefcase under his arm and lurched around to the far side of the table. "The will is in here."

"You're crazy," Harmon shouted. "Don't open that. It's private."

Sherman was already rummaging through the miscellaneous files and papers. "Ah, what do you know! Here it is!" And with a flourish, Sherman pulled out the signed document.

"I don't know why Jacob cut you out of his will, Harmon, old man. Had he lived another week, he might have put you back in. It must have seemed very arbitrary and unjust. So, you just pretended the will was missing."

Anna's mouth was agape. "How do you know that?"

"Harmon said he was in the new will, but that couldn't be true. Harmon, you see, signed as a witness. And, as he himself told me, you can't witness a will in which you inherit."

The Doc's Last Lunch (page 33)—Sherman went to the doctor's refrigerator and opened the freezer section. "No ice in the ice tray. Just as I suspected. That's how the doctor's last patient got the kettle not to whistle until 12:35. He filled it with ice cubes and put it on a low flame."

"You mean the killer was the patient I saw leaving?"

"Yes. This nut case, as Ms. Gould so aptly put it, was clever enough to make the crime appear to have happened later. He rigged the kettle, opened the tuna, and sliced the apple. He probably even moved the body into the kitchen."

"That's a cute theory," Wilson said. "But . . ."

"Note the oxidated flesh of the apple." Sherman pointed to the browned fruit, then to the fruit knife in the victim's hand. "If the doctor had cut the apple himself, as we're meant to believe, it couldn't have turned so brown so soon. We discovered the body just minutes after he supposedly cut it."

A Halloween Homicide (page 35)—"The accident was definitely staged," Sherman whispered to his friend. "Someone came in the back way, probably bringing the mask and candy, too. Miss Cleghorn was pushed down the stairs and the scene was set. You were meant to come to the exact conclusion you came to."

"Get off it," Wilson growled. "Every death isn't a murder."

"Those pearls at the top of the stairs? You try slipping on them and see if they stay in place. In a real accident, the string would break. At the very least, the pearls would have slid out from under her feet."

"Oh." Wilson took a deep breath. "I see your point."

"If I were you, I'd question Emma. We never mentioned that Miss Wilson had fallen down the stairs, and yet she instantly assumed it."

The Commercial Break Break-In (page 38)—"You don't have to get snippy," Sherman said. His feelings were hurt, but not enough to keep him from showing off. "First off, this was an inside job. When Trent stepped on the ladder, it crunched through the snow, proving that it had never supported any weight."

Amelia Warner gasped. "You're saying it was one of us? Let me tell you, Mr. Sherman Holmes . . . "

Sherman scurried behind Trent, as if looking for protection. And then, in a split second, he pulled the revolver from the guard's holster.

Sherman trained the gun on the startled guard. "It couldn't have been someone from inside the house because there were no snowy footprints leading to the door. So whoever put up the ladder didn't come out of the house or go back into it. If you'll check Mr. Trent's coat pockets, I believe you'll find the jewelry and cash."

"Me?" Trent bristled. "I'm the one who discovered the ladder."

"After you planted it there. While we thought you were so bravely searching the upstairs rooms, you were actually robbing them."

An Alarming Jewel Heist (page 41)—"The alarm didn't catch anyone." Zach still sounded angry

"Yes, it did. Tell me, Zach. How long do you think the thief took to clean you out?"

Zach glanced around the showroom. "A minimum of five minutes, probably ten."

"And yet, when the police got here two minutes after the alarm, the burglar was already gone."

"Yeah." Zach scratched his head. "That's impossible."

"Not if the burglar was already inside. After we left, he came out of hiding and took what he wanted. He set off the alarm when he left the shop, not when he arrived."

"You say he. It was a man?"

"It was Sam Wells. He was the only person we didn't actually see exiting the shop. He must have hidden in a closet or behind a counter until after we left. It had to be him. No one else could have come in while we were still here, not without setting off the door buzzer."

All in the Family (page 44)—"George Gleason didn't have a chance to ask any questions," Wilson explained confidently. "He saw the victim's bloody head and the rifle and assumed Lovett had been shot. But, of course, he hadn't been."

"And that indicates his innocence?"

"Absolutely. He's protecting his kids."

"Which is exactly what he wants us to think."

Wilson frowned. "What are you talking about?"

"Gleason wants us to think he's making a false confession. He knew we'd pick up on his mistake and strike him off our suspect list. Very clever of him."

"How do you figure that?"

"Because he knew Lovett had been killed last night. Lovett is often here early, but he rarely stays past noon. An innocent man would have assumed Lovett had been killed this morning. Only the person who telephoned him last night and lured him here would know when Lovett had been ambushed and killed."

Blue Carbuncle, the Sequel (page 47)—Sherman would have loved to do a full crime scene examination, but it really wasn't necessary. As soon as he'd discovered his loss, he knew the most probable suspect.

He checked his address book, got into his car, and drove to Dora Treat's house, arriving just minutes after the nurse practitioner herself.

"You did it as a challenge," he said as she answered the door. "I know you wouldn't really steal from me."

Dora looked confused for a second. "How did you know . . . " A variety of emotions seemed to cross her face. The last one looked a lot like resignation. "Yes, of course, a challenge. I thought it might be nice to have another 'Adventure of the Blue Carbuncle.'"

"Oh, I knew it had to be a joke," Sherman said with obvious relief.

"Of course." Reaching into her purse, she returned the small, blue gemstone. "What gave me away?"

"You were in a hurry, correct? Any second and I might have walked in and caught you. And yet you searched through all three boxes."

"And that eliminated the others?"

"Both Sam and Buddy saw me put the carbuncle in the red box. But you weren't in the room at the time. You were the only one who didn't know which box held the carbuncle."

The Poker from Nowhere (page 50)—The patrolman ushered the daughter and the younger son into the house, while Sherman stood on the brick path and smiled benignly at the victim's oldest child.

"Does your house have a fireplace, Jason?"

"As a matter of fact, it doesn't. But Jennifer's got one. And I think there's one in Gary's apartment."

"Is that why you chose a poker as the murder weapon? We can trace where you bought it, you know."

"What are you talking about?" Jason's voice rose in anger. "Are you accusing me of stabbing my father?'

"I am. How do you know he was stabbed?"

Jason stopped and looked confused. "The poker. You said he was killed with a poker."

"That's right. And if I told a dozen people that a man had been killed with a poker, I expect the full dozen would assume he'd been hit—bludgeoned, if you will. It's by far the easier, more common way to use the instrument. And yet, you somehow knew he'd been stabbed."

Buddy Brown (page 53)—"I don't want to turn you in," Sherman said softly.

It was two days later and the family was walking away from the burial site, heading back to the funeral home's limousine parked by the cemetery's gravel road.

Sherman had maneuvered his way to Susan's side. They were out of earshot of the others and would be for the next minute or two.

"I don't want to turn you in," he repeated. "Why did you do it?"

"For the kids," said Susan. Her tone was eerily calm. "You saw how it was. All the time he pushed them down, controlled everything. Maybe now they can live their own lives. Me, too," she added as an afterthought.

"You poisoned his napkin." Sherman had to show her that he knew. "Every time he went to wipe his mouth, he inhaled a little poison. Then after he collapsed and no one was looking, you replaced it with a clean napkin. That's what I noticed. A clean napkin—that should have been covered with butter."

"You can't prove it," Susan said with a thin smile. "Even if you dig up the body and check it for poison, that napkin no longer exists. You can't prove a thing."

The Ring-Stealing Ring (page 56)—Zach eyed his old friend with evident distrust.

"Sherman, if you can prove they stole the ring, why didn't you do it ten minutes ago?"

"I would have proved it earlier, but legally we couldn't search them."

"Search them?" Zach was livid. "What are you talking about? The police just did search them."

Sherman was used to holding his temper and being polite. "Before you and I left the back room," he said calmly, "all three suspects were chewing gum, correct?"

Zach thought for a second. "Correct."

"And yet, when it came time to eat the hamburgers, only two of them removed the gum from their mouths. What happened to the third kid's gum?"

"I don't know. Maybe he swallowed it."

Without another word of speculation, Sherman walked into the back room. Kneeling down, he checked under the table and the chairs. "Here it is," he said, lifting up a chair and showing the underside. "Timmy's chair. I'm also willing to bet this is Timmy's gum stuck on the bottom and your ring stuck in the middle of it. I won't touch it, in case there's a partial print."

Mrs. Krenshaw's Spare Key (page 59)—Mrs. Krenshaw was confused. "Of course I won't like the answer, Mr. Holmes. It's never nice to find out someone is a thief."

"Well, on that score you don't have to worry. Neither Hank nor Edgar stole the vase. You did."

"Me?"

Sherman nodded. "I assume you did this as a dry run, to see if your little scheme would pass muster when you tell it to the police. It won't, dear lady."

"What do you mean? Why would I steal my own vase?"

"For the insurance money. Since the vase was just appraised by an expert, your homeowner's insurance would have to pay."

The elderly woman scowled. "All right. Where did I screw up? Did you see me from your window?"

"No. Those footprints in the snow gave you away."

"How? I wore a pair of my late husband's shoes."

"But there was only one set. If the thief took the key, unlocked the door, and later returned the key to the flowerpot, then there would have been two sets of prints, one when he took the key and one when he returned it. The thief—you—made those prints to throw suspicion on someone else. Then you used your own key to get in and out."

Check the Brakes (page 62)—"You can't know who it is." Given Sherman's record, Sergeant Wilson hated to disagree, but this was one time when he saw no possible explanation. "Are you saying their alibis won't check out?"

"Not at all," said Sherman. "They might indeed. Chuck might well have been on the phone the entire time. The same might be true for Tyrone. As for Dominique, if we didn't believe Mrs. Watts's testimony, then we could check the time stamp on the video recorder. I assume that they're all telling the truth."

"Well, then, when were the brake lines cut?"

Sherman paused for effect. "Before dinner, old boy."

"Before . . . ?" Wilson had to smile. "You're slipping, old boy. Mr. Graves only announced his will at the dinner table. Before dinner, no one had a reason to want him dead."

Now it was Sherman's time to smile. "If you were Graves and you were changing your will, who would you go to?"

"A lawyer, of course."

"And who was Milton Graves's lawyer? His niece, Dominique."

"You're right." Wilson slapped his leg. "We'll check that will. If Dominique drew it up, then she goes to the top of our list—the only suspect who knew ahead of time about the inheritance."

Death of a Swinger (page 65)—Did you fellows all get along?" Sherman asked in his most innocuous tone. "Was Bobby a good friend?"

The roommates exchanged glances. ' Well . . . " Julio hemmed. "Bobby had this habit of stealing girls. He never messed with my Angie, but I heard from other guys. He got this perverse pleasure from going after girls who were already dating."

"I doubt that was true," said Thad Killian. "Just gossip, you know."

"Then why did you kill him?" asked Sherman.

Thad chuckled. "What do you mean?"

"You killed him, Thad. You cut the rope and threw it off the cliff. Then, when Bobby showed up to swim, you pushed him off the cliff."

Thad stopped chuckling. "That's ridiculous."

"Your story was ridiculous. Bobby didn't swing on that rope as you said. If he had, the severed rope end would have landed on top of his body or beside it. But the rope end was found underneath him. He couldn't have been swinging on it when he fell."

THOMAS P. STANWICK

The Case of the Wells Fargo Money (page 73)—
Suppose Acker is lying. Then, from his second statement, he was out of town at the time of the robbery and Crowley is lying. If Crowley is lying, they are all using the lying code, including Barrington. If Barrington is lying, however, then Acker was in town at the time of the robbery. Thus, if Acker is lying, he was both in and out of town at the time of the robbery. This is impossible. Acker is therefore telling the truth.

Since Acker is telling the truth, he knows where the money is, and Barrington is using the lying code. Not everyone is using the lying code, so Crowley is telling the truth and doesn't know where the money is. Barrington may or may not know the location of the money.

A Slaying in the North End (page 76)—Neither Diskin nor Foster is the leader (4). Since the leader is married (3), he isn't O'Keefe (6), and since he plays poker Tuesday nights (4), he isn't Jensen either (2). The leader therefore is Lyons.

The leader and the killer are different men (1), so Lyons isn't the killer. Neither Jensen nor O'Keefe is the killer (5). Since the killer has a sister (5), he isn't Foster either (3). Therefore the killer is Diskin.

Bad Day for Bernidi (page 79)—Stanwick suspects Bernidi himself.

According to Bernidi's story, he lay down in the narrow space behind one of the display counters. His face was to the wall, and the lower wooden panels of the counter would have obstructed his vision even if he had turned. Since he supposedly did not arise until after the thief left, he could not have known that the thief used a burlap sack.

Business had been bad for Bernidi. He fabricated the entire robbery for the insurance money and was sent to prison for his trouble.

An Unaccountable Death (page 82)—Morey said that he had touched nothing after finding Lombard in his lit office, yet when Walker arrived he had to snap on the lights. Morey later confessed to killing Lombard after the accountant had found tax fraud and threatened blackmail.

The Case of the Purloined Painting (page 84)—Had an outsider broken the patio door glass to get in, the glass would have been on the floor inside, not out on the patio where Stanwick found it. The glass had therefore been broken from the inside.

The maid later confessed to being an accomplice in the theft, and both thief and painting were found.

The Week of the Queen Anne Festival (page 86)—All three are lying, and Thursday alone is a festival day.

If Chiswick's statement is true, then they are all liars, including Chiswick. He would thus be a liar telling the truth, which is impossible. Chiswick's statement is therefore false, and Chiswick is a liar. At least one clause of his compound statement is therefore false.

Since Chiswick's statement is false, Green's claim that it is true is also false, and Green is also a liar. Thus his other statement that Tuesday is a festival day is false. Hunter's first statement is false, since Chiswick and Green are both lying. Hunter is therefore also a liar, and Wednesday is not a festival day.

Thus, all three are liars. This means the first clause of Chiswick's statement is true. For the statement as a whole to be false, which it is, the remaining clause must be false, so Friday is not a festival day either.

Tuesday, Wednesday, Thursday, and Friday are the only possible festival days. Since at least one must be a festival day, and Tuesday, Wednesday, and Friday are not festival days, then Thursday must be the only festival day.

Death of a Con Man (page 89)—Cochran is the killer. There are several proofs, of which this is one:

SOLUTIONS
Thomas P. Stanwick

The second statements of Cannon and Cochran contradict each other. Therefore one is true and one is false. Since each suspect is making one true and one false statement, the first statement of one of them, denying guilt, is true, and the other denial is false. Thus, one of them is the killer.

The killer cannot be Cannon, since both his statements would then be false. Therefore the killer must be Cochran.

The Case of the Edgemore Street Shooting (page 91)—Kravitz said that Walder was approached from behind and shot before he could see his assailant. If this were true, Walder would have been shot in the back, not in the chest.

Kravitz was convicted of the murder.

Death Comes to the Colonel (page 93)—Since the colonel's phone rang, it must have been on the hook. According to George Huddleston, however, the colonel had had a sudden seizure while dialing, and nothing had been touched since. If this were true, the phone would have been dropped, and would not have been found back on the hook.

Huddleston was later convicted of poisoning the colonel for inheritance money.

Stanwick Finds the Magic Words (page 96)—All green elephants drink martinis at five (statement 6). But members of the Diagonal Club drink martinis only at four (3). Therefore no green elephants are members of the Diagonal Club. But only green elephants who are members of the Diagonal Club can wear striped ties (5). Thus no green elephants can wear striped ties.

All friends of winged armadillos, however, wear striped ties (1). Therefore no green elephants are friends of winged armadillos. But all who eat pickled harmonicas are friends of winged armadillos (4). Thus no green elephants eat pickled harmonicas. But only those who eat pickled harmonicas can enter a chocolate courtroom (2). Therefore (and these are the magic words) no green elephants can enter a chocolate courtroom.

SOLUTIONS
Thomas P. Stanwick

Inspector Walker Feels the Heat (page 99)—Ellis alone is guilty of assaulting the deputy mayor.

Suppose Chase is guilty. Then Heath is innocent (4). But then Decker is both guilty (1) and innocent (5), which is impossible. Therefore Chase is innocent. Since Chase is innocent, Mullaney is innocent (2). Therefore Heath is innocent (3). (If Heath were guilty, then Mullaney would be guilty, but Mullaney is innocent.) Since Heath is innocent, Decker is innocent (5).

Each member of the gang of four is therefore innocent. Since at least one of the five suspects is guilty, the guilty man must be Ellis.

Stanwick Visits Scotland Yard (page 102)—James Malcolm stole the documents.

If he and his wife had gone to the theatre, the ticket-taker would have kept half of each ticket he tore. Thus, when Malcolm carelessly produced both halves of two torn theater tickets, his alibi was proved false.

The Explorer's Tale (page 105)—Justin mentioned seeing tigers in the African jungle. Africa has no wild tigers.

The Case of the Reindeer Spies (page 107)—"Dasher" can't be Cantrell, who vacations with him, or Bircham or Delmarin, who are single. Since he has never left the state, he can't be Ephesos either. Therefore "Dasher" is Abelardo. Similarly, "Donder" can't be the single Bircham or Delmarin. Since he has a brother, he can't be Ephesos. Therefore "Donder" is Cantrell.

The retired, worldly Ephesos cannot be the dissatisfied "Cupid" or the provincial "Comet." Therefore he is "Dancer." And the well-traveled Bircham cannot be "Comet," so he is "Cupid." Delmarin is "Comet."

Stanwick and the Accidental Thief (page 110)—When Stanwick walked by the ladies' coin purses earlier, he was able to observe the price tags, implying that they were on the outside of the purses. When Carpenter examined the coin purse carried out by Celia Leonard, however, he found its price tag tucked inside, where she had hidden it.

The McPherson-McTavish Mystery (page 113)—McTavish's golf bag is only scuffed. If he had dragged it across the moor to the knoll, as he claimed, it would also have had the moor's sticky red clay adhering to it, as it had adhered to Stanwick's shoes. The missing knife had nothing to do with the crime.

McTavish was convicted of murdering his neighbor over a land dispute and then attempting to frame McPherson.

Murder in a London Flat (page 116)—Since the gunman was not in London the week before the crime, he could not be Llewellyn, Merrick, or Halifax. Therefore the gunman is Cross. Neither Merrick nor Halifax, who kept the flat under surveillance, is the innocent bystander, so he must be Llewellyn.

Llewellyn knows Merrick, but not the lookout, so the lookout must be Halifax. Merrick, by elimination, must be the planner.

The Matter of the McAlister Murders (page 119)—If Collins's statement had been false, then Byran and Derrick would have been the guilty ones. Collins would then have been an innocent man telling a lie. Therefore Collins's statement was true, and he was innocent.

SOLUTIONS
Thomas P. Stanwick

The other innocent one must have been either Byran or Derrick, as Collins stated. Therefore Addler was guilty and his statement was false, so Byran was innocent and Derrick was guilty. Addler and Derrick were therefore the guilty ones.

Death in the Garage (page 121)

Death in the Garage (page 121)—If McCarthy had committed suicide, he probably would have taken the pills soon before succumbing to asphyxiation. Since the pills took effect so quickly, he would have had to take them while already seated in the car.

To take several large lozenges, however, he would have needed something to wash them down with, and no beverage container was found in the car. Stanwick therefore believes that the case is one of murder made to resemble suicide.

Murder at the Chessboard (page 124)

Murder at the Chessboard (page 124)—Rimbach's story implies that the murder occurred during a game of monochromatic chess. In this form of chess, the knight, a piece that moves only from a black square to a white square or from a white square to a black square, can never move.

In the position on the dead man's chessboard, however, a knight had moved to the center of the board. Rimbach is therefore lying. He committed the murder and then set the scene in the study, but in setting up the chess position made a fatal error.

INSPECTOR FORSOOTH

▬▬▬

Murder Around The Clock (page 131)—

1) Who killed Bruce Berringer?

The killer was Sean McGillicuddy, the milkman.

2) How can the other suspects be ruled out?

There are two ways to solve the murder—the hard way and the easy way. First off, we note that when Berringer wrote "1:30 hence," he wasn't referring to the time of the shooting; he was referring to what the position of the clocks would be 1 hour and 30 minutes hence. (As discussed in the Q&A, the "hence" meant "in the future," not "therefore.")

The hard way to solve the crime is to use a semaphore code directly. At approximately 2:37 Mountain Time (the time zone in Bogusville), it would be 3:37 in Chicago, the first of the seven clocks on the wall. But if you look at the hand positions at 3:37, you'll see they are quite close to the flag positions of the letter "M" in the semaphore alphabet (right arm at a slight angle to the left, left arm almost straight out to the right).

Now apply the same logic to each of the seven clocks. At 2:37 Mountain Time, it would be 10:37 in Paris, which corresponds roughly with the "I" in semaphore. And so on for Los Angeles ("L"=1:37), Cairo ("K"=11:37), Mexico City ("M"=3:37), Caracas ("A"=5:37), and New York ("N"=4:37). The correspondences aren't all perfect (Berringer was a dying man, after all), but there is a strong match between the indicated times and letters. Together, the letters spell out "MILKMAN." Berringer was identifying Sean McGillicuddy, the milkman, as his killer.

But you didn't need to know semaphore to figure this case out. The "easy" way is to observe that Chicago and Mexico City are in the same time zone, meaning that they would signify the same letter in the semaphore alphabet! Right away we know that Berringer couldn't have been referring to Dowling or Walters (the only two suspects whose last names have seven letters), because neither name has any repeated letters. The only conclusion is that Berringer, true to his approach to life, must have been identifying his killer by using the man's profession, not his name.

Wouldn't you know that each of the five professions— CATERER, PLUMBER, MILKMAN, REFEREE, and MAÎTRE D'— has seven letters? However, we can rule out four of them as follows:

Using the same logic as we used earlier for the names Dowling and Walters, the killer couldn't have been the plumber or the maître d', because each letter in those job titles is distinct. Similarly, the position of the clocks couldn't possibly be identifying the referee (four e's), or the caterer (two sets of repeated letters). "MILKMAN" was the only job that had one and only one repeated letter, spelling doom for Sean McGillicuddy.

McGillicuddy thought he had stumbled onto the perfect alibi when first questioned concerning his whereabouts at 1:30 a.m., a time when he in fact was out with several others who could vouch for him. But at Interactive Mysteries, we always get our man.

Timing Is Everything (page 138)—

1) Who killed James Hooligan?
Muriel Huxley.

2) Explain the key elements of timing in this case.
First of all, the bathroom light of Hooligan's case simply burned out; it bore no relationship to the crime! (Before you cry "foul play," let me say that this little nugget came from a real case. Unlikely, but true.)

As for the method, Muriel had cut the combination lock off a couple of days before the murder, and had replaced it with an identical-looking combination lock. Her husband never realized the change had taken place, because he didn't have any occasion to get into the toolshed in the meantime. Muriel also took the rifle out at that earlier time. She killed Hooligan prior to the meeting between her husband, Martinez, and Plotz, and she ditched the rifle in the woods, just as she had ditched the bolt cutters a couple of days before. But the extra rust on the bolt cutters suggested they might have been outside longer than just one night. A fatal mistake.

A couple of other small "timing" clues point Muriel's way. Remember that when she came down with the news of Hooligan's death, she had just finished planting all those daffodil bulbs. But she couldn't have been planting all that long; it was still morning, and besides, she had just heard the radio announcement, which presumably had been mentioned many times on her all-news station. It follows that she had been doing her gardening for several days despite her being "locked out" of the shed, taking advantage of her husband's preoccupation with the kickback scheme.

3) What was the missing piece of evidence that tied the murderer to the crime?

The missing piece of evidence was the other lock—the one Muriel Huxley bought to replace the lock she cut off with the bolt cutters! (If you guessed the burned-out lightbulb in Hooligan's bathroom, take credit for some good sleuthing.)

And just why did Muriel kill James Hooligan? Because she and her husband were getting along dreadfully, and she saw a way out of the marriage, the blackmailing, everything. She knew that her husband and/or his henchmen would be blamed for the crime, precisely because she had no apparent motive. Unfortunately for poor Muriel, she was now going to a place where someone else would hold the key to the lock.

The Piano Requital (page 145)—

1) Who killed Gilbert von Stade?

Vivien Frechette. She felt she was every bit von Stade's equal (as evidenced by her strong performance of the complicated piece he had chosen), but she never got anywhere near the recognition he did. That's right: Gilbert von Stade was the victim of professional jealousy.

2) What was the method, and why did it work?

Just before the beginning of the show, Frechette laced a couple of black keys in the upper (right-hand) region of the piano with a combination of batrachotoxin and DMSO (dimethyl sulfoxide, in case you want to impress your friends). Note that she didn't have to go to South America to find the poison; it is available at various medical labs in the United States, for example. And all it took was a few drops.

As discussed in the question-and-answer session, DMSO plays a vital role because of its property of being quickly absorbed into the body. DMSO is capable of carrying other compounds into the bloodstream along with it, even if the person's only contact with the mixture is with the surface of the skin. However, one of DMSO's common side effects is that it leaves the user with a garlicky taste in his mouth! (Note: It was quite unlikely that von Stade's garlic breath came from something he ate. After all, he was in the men's room between the dinner and the performance, and he could have used any of the items there to deal with the garlic taste that he plainly disliked.)

The reason why Heinrich Albertson wasn't killed is that his piece (Etude in C major) uses almost no black keys, whereas von Stade's piece (Etude in G flat) is commonly referred to as Chopin's "black-key" étude, such is its emphasis on flats and sharps. Because the poisonous solution was a skimmed-on liquid, von Stade might have noticed that something was amiss, but, being the seasoned professional that he was, he evidently concluded that the show must go on.

In theory, the fact that the show went on would have boded

poorly for Vivien Frechette, who followed von Stade in the evening's program. But von Stade had basically wiped the keys clean with his hands; in addition, Frechette's first piece, being slow and melancholy, was much longer than the others, which, coupled with the disruption following von Stade's death, would have given the remaining solution time to evaporate under the stage lights! These factors all but eliminated the possibility that a lethal or even toxic dosage could have made its way into her bloodstream. (Also, her first piece uses almost exclusively the white keys in the lower ranges of the keyboard, as opposed to the higher-pitched flats and sharps of the black-key étude.)

Theoretically, it was possible that someone who wasn't familiar with the music was trying to kill Heinrich Albertson instead, but the only person who was unfamiliar with sheet music was Marla Albertson; however, she was still very much in love with her husband, and had no apparent reason to do him in.

And that's a wrap.

The Valentine's Day Massacre (page 152)—

1) Who killed Rudy Marcus?

Daphne Nagelson killed Rudy Marcus.

2) Rudy's personality played a role in his demise, in two distinct ways. Name them.

First, and most obviously, Rudy's philandering is what got him in trouble. Second, Rudy was a victim of the accountant in him. When he bought Mary Stahl a gold necklace in California, he had it shipped home, thereby avoiding the state sales tax. Unfortunately for Rudy, when his business trip was delayed, the UPS delivery person arrived with his package before he was home to receive it. The delivery person left either the package or a little slip of paper (we don't really know which) in Rudy's vestibule. Whatever was left bore the markings of a California boutique, which didn't go unnoticed by Daphne when she stopped by to drop off her present to Rudy. At the time, she doubtless thought the present was for her, hence the smile on her face. When she got the emerald brooch instead, she may have been delighted to receive it, but she immediately knew that Rudy was a two-timer. (The fact that Rudy's trip was delayed also explains why Cornelia did not hear Mary Stahl's message. Because Rudy never called Cornelia while he was gone to tell her of his changed plans, she ended her housesitting on the 12th, not the 13th.)

3) The testimony of two particular people would prove very helpful in bringing the guilty party to justice. Which two people?

The people who would prove helpful in bringing the guilty party to justice are Mrs. Wheelock, who could confirm that Daphne had visited Rudy's home the day before the murder, and the delivery person, who could confirm that the slip of paper (or package) had been left prior to Daphne's arrival. The combination of these two testimonies would have been important in establishing Daphne's guilt.

Where There's A Will (page 159)—

1) Who killed Marion Webster?

The killer was Gwen.

2) Where was the murder weapon hidden after the crime?

Before the murder, Gwen had hollowed out one of the thick reference books in her father's study. That's where she placed the murder weapon immediately following the killing. It didn't occur to the bungling first team of investigators to look within the study itself. (You did better, I'm sure. It's an old trick.) At some point she had a chance to go in and replace the hollow book with a real one.

3) Which of the children was Webster going to treat harshly in his revised will? (One of them is the killer!)

Marion Webster had decided to change his will to give Gwen a fake necklace ("put on ice") instead of the family heirloom. That was her motive. The others to be treated harshly by their father were Herbert (who had a fine "past as a lad," but who had disappointed his father thereafter) and Dorothy (whose library donations were going to be reduced).

Note that of the three losers in Webster's to-be-revised will, only Gwen's whereabouts were not accounted for. She alone had motive and opportunity.

The "winners" included Eugene (Gene), as tipped off by Webster saying that "Gene rates income"—meaning that he should receive the bond portfolio. The other two winners were Biff and Laura, who benefited from their father's saying that "funding for 'libraries' would increase." Laura (late September) was a Libra and Biff (April 1) was an Aries. The "signs getting crossed" was a reference to the fact that the word "libraries" forces the two signs of the zodiac to share the letter "a." And that's a wrap!

The Overhead Smash (page 164)—

1) Who killed Manny Heitz? What was the murder scenario?

Roger Dant killed Manny Heitz. Dant arrived at Heitz's residence before the 11:00 match and the two got into an argument. The result was that Dant knocked Heitz out and took his place as a linesman. (With sunglasses and a visor, the disguise was made easier. The only people who would have known the difference were too far away. Note also that Dant and Heitz were about the same size.) Heitz was left bound and gagged until after the match. When Dant returned, the two got into another struggle, one that resulted in Heitz's death.

The reason the two got into an argument in the first place was that Dant wanted Chris de la Harpe to win the tennis match. Heitz wasn't willing to be bribed, so Dant decided to take matters into his own hands—making bad calls in de la Harpe's favor to facilitate the upset.

2) What was the crucial piece of evidence that the killer tried to cover up? Why was his effort doomed to failure?

The crucial piece of evidence against Dant was that his sneakers had clay on them from the stadium court at Forest Hills. The year was 1975, and the U.S. Open was being played on clay for the first time. That year, the early men's matches were two out of three sets, not three out of five, which is why the Molotov/de la Harpe match was so short, which in turn enabled Dant to be there for the whole match and still make it to Heitz's house and then the public courts by 1:00 p.m. Also, this explains my "highly misleading" answer to Question #4, in which I note that Heitz lived 15 minutes away from the National Tennis Center at Flushing Meadows (where the U.S. Open moved in 1978). Had I wanted to be more helpful, I would have added that he lived right next to the stadium at Forest Hills! (By the way, the "political intrigue" of that particular U.S. Open was the fact that Martina Navratilova announced her defection to the United States!)

Dant realized that after he killed Heitz, he was in big trouble. He therefore scampered to the local public courts, which were also clay (technically Har-Tru, a green, granular, clay-like surface). By picking up a game, Dant found someone who could vouch for his whereabouts. He also made sure someone noticed his vanity plate. (As noted during the question-and-answer session, New York license plates were orange before the bicentennial year of 1976, when they went to a more conventional red and blue lettering on a white background.) Most important of all, Dant was able to get Har-Tru granules on his sneakers, covering up the fact that he had been on the stadium court.

What Dant hadn't counted on was that Manny Heitz was wearing brand-new sneakers! The absence of Har-Tru granules on the soles of Heitz's sneakers proved he hadn't been at the 11:00 match after all.

3) Name one person whom the prosecution would surely want as a witness for their side.

One person who could have served as a witness for the prosecution was Tracy Molotov. He got a close look at Dant, and despite the visor and sunglasses, he would have been unlikely to forget his face!

Pier for the Course (page 171)—

1) Who killed Bart Strunk?
David Willoughby.

2) Who killed Wayne Metzger?
Again, David Willoughby.

3) How was Metzger killed? You must be specific as to how the crime was perpetrated.

The conspiracy was between senior vice president Wayne Metzger and vice president David Willoughby. Metzger pressured Willoughby into shooting Bart Strunk so that he (Metzger) could take over the reins of the company.

But Willoughby insisted on having an alibi. He agreed to shoot Strunk just as he was finishing his caramel apple. The plan was that Metzger would then place the apple core in a cup of water—this would prevent the apple from "aging," as it would if left in the air, and would make it seem as though Strunk had been shot at a time when Willoughby wasn't in the area. Metzger agreed, the idea being that Willoughby would leave the pier area for a remote site, at which point Metzger would wait a little while before getting help, then would take the apple out of the water to disguise the time of the killing and provide Willoughby with an alibi.

The only wrinkle was that Willoughby, standing at a point on the shore, killed Strunk a bit too soon—on purpose! Metzger found that the apple was too big to fit in the cup of water, and he therefore hurriedly ate the rest of it himself! This is precisely what Willoughby had anticipated. He knew he had a chance to kill two birds with one stone (ultimately he felt angry at being Metzger's flunky for so many years), and he had taken the opportunity to place peanut oil on the outside of Strunk's caramel apple at its widest point—when, ostensibly, he was checking Metzger's food to make sure he had a ham sandwich instead of peanut butter and jelly. The taste of the peanut oil was obscured by the caramel, and, of course, Strunk consumed it without any side effects. But Metzger's intense allergy to peanut oil (a well-known and very serious condition) caused his larynx to tighten up within mere seconds of its ingestion. Metzger had time to place the apple in the water cup, but that's about it. He never made it off the pier.

The final touch was that Willoughby made sure he found the bodies first, confident that the others would be distracted by their own projects. When he arrived with Sharon Sturgis, he saw to it that she attended to Wayne Metzger, so that he could attend to Strunk. Willoughby simply removed the apple from the cup of water, thereby creating the illusion that his alibi depended on.

That's it!

SHERLOCK HOLMES

Code One (page 183)—The numbers represent the vowels, 2 = A, 3 = E, etc. Then by breaking the message up into words, it reads: Tomorrow I will steal the crown jewels. This will be my greatest triumph.

Age Old Question (page 184)—Fish 22 years. Hill 33 years. Giles 66 years.

Spending Spree (page 185)—£48.

Lestrade in Stride (page 186)—12 points. 5 points were awarded for first place, 2 points for second, and 1 point for third.

Aston Avenue Robberies (page 187)—Number 5 Aston Avenue.

A Threatening Gift (page 188)—A coffin.

Identify the Witnesses (page 189)—Andrew Richards, Frank Andrews, Richard Franks.

Stake Out the Professor (page 190)—No. 24.
The pattern: 4 x 4 = 16 – 4 = 12 ÷ 4 = 3 + 4 = 7 x 4 = 28 – 4 = 24

If the Coat Fits . . . (page 192)—Lestrade was wearing the overcoat belonging to Holmes, while Holmes wore Watson's and Watson wore Lestrade's.

The Butler Did It (page 193)—The wine in the smaller glass was one-sixth of the total liquid, while the wine in the larger glass was two-ninths of the total. Add these together to reveal that the wine was seven-eighteenths. Therefore, the poison content has to be eleven-eighteenths.

In Training (page 194)—

7	4	8	= 19
2	9	5	= 16
6	3	1	= 10
‖	‖	‖	⟍
15	16	14	17

Which Way Did He Go? (page 195)—West.

An Upstanding Victim (page 196)—6 feet, 4 inches.

Reporting a Crime (page 197)—Lestrade wrote 42 pages, Holmes wrote 37 pages, and Watson 20 pages.

Trapped! (page 198)—41 and 28 (69), 46 and 33 (79), 21 and 8 (29).

Going Off in All Directions (page 199)—Holmes was travelling to Manchester, Watson to Edinburgh, and Lestrade to Brighton.

Killer in the Club (page 200)—Wilson. The code numbers were devised by taking each letter of the member's surname and relating each one to its place in the alphabet. A = 1, B = 2, etc. Wilson consists of the 23rd, 9th, 12th, 19th, 15th, and 14th. Added together they make 92.

Riddle Me This . . . (page 201)—William Ewart Gladstone (the Prime Minister).

One Measly Diamond (page 202)—38 diamonds.

Who Rode Tinkerbell? (page 203)—Lestrade rode Tinkerbell, while Martin rode Spring Goddess.

Five in a Row (page 204)—Inspector Lestrade occupied seat number 39, while Sergeant Baxter had seat number 37.

Dinner at Lady McBride's (page 205)—The guests arrived as follows: 7:30 Lord Winterbottom. 7:45 Sir Harry Trump. 7:50 Lady Barclay. 7:59 Sir John Penn. 8:05 Lady James. 8:20 Lord Hadden.

On the Brighton Train (page 206)—
Mr. Baker/Andrews Street.
Mr. Andrews/Dawson Street.
Mr. Clark/Easton Street.

Mr. Dawson/Baker Street.
Mr. Easton/Clark Street.

Miss Aldridge's Boarders (page 207)—28 guests.

He Said, She Said (page 208)—Mary.

Members of the Committee (page 209)—Hopkins is the vice-chairman. White is the chairman. Smythe is the secretary. Knight is the treasurer.

Four Into Sixteen (page 210)—Here is one possibility.

Backwater's End (page 211)—The gardener is the butler's great-grandson.

A Scion in Danger (page 212)—Death shall take Master Sharp today.

Who Did What? (page 213)—Barnett: Mustache. Gold watch. Wetherby: Beard. Cigar case. Black: Clean-shaven. Wallet.

Moriarty's Haul (page 214)—132 diamonds.

Forge On! (page 215)—One forger had £141 and the other had £86.

Mint Condition (page 216)—27 coins.

Well-Armed (page 217)—Fingers carried the club.

A Shot Rang Out (page 218)—11:45 AM.

Not Quite Cricket (page 219)—Holmes was wearing Lestrade's jersey, Watson was wearing Smith's, Lestrade wore Watson's, and Smith wore Holmes'.

They Had It Covered (page 220)—5 miles.

Caught Redhanded (page 221)—Moriarty had £28, Bloggs £15, Norris £20, Hunt £31.

Moriarty in Top Security (page 222)—

Tibbs	Milne	Kidd	Pearce
Gunn	Moriarty	Robb	Conn
Hobbs	Webb	Field	Little

Foiled Again! (page 224)—Monday: Disguised as a prison officer. Tuesday: Tried to tunnel from his cell. Wednesday: Tried to bribe a prison officer. Thursday: Tried to join the work party. Friday: Exchanged identity with a visitor.

Mystery Crate (page 225)—The number of the last crate is 38. The number on each crate is found by adding together the number of the two crates directly above it.

Something's Fishy (page 226)—The Madisons lived at No. 1 and lost the decanter. The Newtons lived at No. 5 and lost the gold watch. The O'Connors lived at No. 3 and lost the £50.

INDEX